THE MAN BENEATH THE GIFT

THE MAN
BENEATH
THE GIFT

The Story of My Life

by Father Ralph A. DiOrio
with Donald Gropman

WILLIAM MORROW AND COMPANY, INC.
New York   1980

Library of Congress Cataloging in Publication Data

DiOrio, Ralph A., 1930-
  The man beneath the gift.

  Includes index.
  1. Catholic Church—Clergy—Biography.
2. Clergy—United States—Biography. 3. Healers—
United States—Biography. I. Gropman, Donald,
joint author. II. Title.
BX4705.D545A35   282'.0924'   [B]   80-17619
ISBN 0-688-03740-2

Printed in the United States of America

5   6   7   8   9   10

BOOK DESIGN BY MICHAEL MAUCERI

FOREWORD

At different times throughout the ages, God has blessed some very special people with a unique gift in order to prove again that He, in His ultimate mercy, is always with us. I know that, for our lifetime, Father Ralph DiOrio is one of His chosen people.

Through this book and other media, Father DiOrio's ministry will, I believe, have an impact in the nation and the world.

Father DiOrio's mother, Molly, first recognized that her son would become a vessel of God when, at the age of fourteen, he decided to enter the priesthood. Her unfaltering faith in him led her to dedicate her life to his ministry.

It was some years after he became a priest that Father DiOrio realized that God had selected him for His special work. His congregation began to tell him of healings that had occurred when he prayed with them. At first Father DiOrio felt they were occasional miracles of God, until the healings became more and more numerous. People were requesting special audiences with him for healing purposes. Since then, thousands of people can testify to physical and spiritual healings initiated through Father DiOrio's services and the God he loves.

I have personally witnessed his remarkable healing gift from God, have been with him at the altar, and believe that his anointment is beyond question. As Father DiOrio passes through the crowds gathered for his blessing, a beautiful aura surrounds him. Outstretched arms and tear-filled eyes follow him in awe. Everyone prays that through Father DiOrio, God will heal and mend their broken bodies, hearts, and spirits. One need only to look upon his face as he reaches out to these stricken people to know that God is walking with him.

But no one realizes better than Father DiOrio that, personally, he is helpless and completely dependent on the Holy Spirit once the miracle of healing begins. God and God alone decides who will be healed.

I've spoken to Father DiOrio just before a mass and have thoroughly enjoyed his magnificent sense of humor and his everyday outlook on life. Then, perhaps just a few minutes after being at the altar, a special presence envelops Father DiOrio, and it's clear that the Holy Spirit is now in *full charge*. His face becomes serene—even his walk is different—and then one knows that God is "ready."

No one ever leaves these services quite the same person who entered. Seeing God perform His miracles through this priest testifies to the Almighty's ability to fulfill every promise to those created in His image. Father DiOrio's awesome love and obedience to the Holy Spirit pervade his every movement and cause him to follow God's teachings unconditionally.

The strong guidance he receives from the Holy Spirit allows him to view people as God does—with ultimate compassion. I know of no one who has accomplished more toward bringing *all* faiths together unto a common love of God. His Godly wisdom has allowed Jews, Protestants, and Catholics alike to recognize that, in each of them, the same God is living equally.

Father DiOrio would be the first to agree that the spiritual healing is the greatest and most important of all. Jesus taught us that if we believe in Him all other forms of healing are possible.

Born unto this family of God, Father Ralph DiOrio accepted his mission—and God smiled.

SARA BUCKNER O'MEARA
Chairperson of the National Board
of Children's Village, U.S.A.,
a project of I.O.I.

CONTENTS

AUTHOR'S NOTE

The contents of this book are not intended to present formal ecclesiastical teachings pertaining to faith and morals, nor do they pretend to render to the reading audience a prescribed ascetic form of spirituality. The sole purpose of this book, which has been written in response to many requests, is to present the authentic facts, events, and circumstances of my life. Moreover, this book contains my personal testimony of God's grace encompassing me. It is my hope that this narration may be seen as a holistic diary which will inspire the reader and dispose him to the recognition of his own genuine vocational calling and to a courageous surrender to be that which God intended him to be. To God be the glory!

"AD MAJOREM DEI GLORIAM"

INTRODUCTION

~~~~~~

You are about to read the story of my life. I have been a Roman Catholic priest since my ordination on June 1, 1957, twenty-three years ago. But until four years ago, it never would have occurred to me to write my autobiography. I didn't think my life was that unusual or that my story would be of interest to very many people. But four years ago, on May 9, 1976, to be exact, God did something to me that changed my life. On that day, He caused me to understand that He had chosen me as a clear channel through which He wished to send His Healing Grace to all His children.

Since that day, in numerous Healing Ministry services, I have witnessed thousands of healings caused by God's Grace as He transmitted it through me. Thousands of men, women, and children have received physical, emotional or spiritual healings during these services.

And since that day when God revealed His plan for me, I have looked back on my life and I have understood that God was always preparing me for His Healing Ministry, that all the events of my life were stepping-stones placed by Him on the pathway to this moment. So the story of my life is the story of how God prepared me to be His clear channel, and I am most grateful to God, my Father.

The Healing Ministry, which is part of the Charismatic Renewal Movement, has taken me to numerous parts of the country where I have conducted healing services. I have also been on radio and television and been featured in many newspaper and magazine articles. One of the results of reaching such a large audience has been a series of requests for information about my life. Many people have asked me to write a book which would tell about the Healing Gifts and also about myself, Father Ralph. With all respect I present such a book now, with the hope that the story of my life as a man and as a Roman Catholic priest will bring my readers closer to God, His Loving Mercy, and His Healing Grace.

The purpose of the pages which follow is to share my story with you, the reader, as an example of how God can use anyone who is willing to surrender himself in the belief that God is alive and God does care. The story will also demonstrate once again that God yearns to use individual persons, and use them distinctively, for the building up of the "Body of Christ."

Every human story reveals a human soul—your soul as well as mine. Every soul has its own story to tell, from the very moment of its conception through the moment of its birth; through the days of living and unto death, the prelude to eternal life.

Each soul's story is rich and complex because life is not an accident. It is not by chance that we live. If our own birth is in tune with the Creator of all birth, of all life, then the unfolding events of our lives are nothing less than the blooming of our souls into the maturity of God's plan.

When God calls a man to vocation, He predisposes the events of that man's life as a prelude to that calling. When we want to trace that prelude, follow that pattern, see the overall design of our lives, we must necessarily start by turning backward to look at our beginnings.

All recollections are precious because they are windows on the past. But perhaps the most precious of all are the memories of early childhood which take us back to our beginnings. The incidents of childhood have great value because it is in them that the patterns of our lives first emerge. Truly, the child is father of the man. I've always believed the child is father of the man in the sense that life's pattern, or God's plan, as I prefer to see it, unfolds at the very beginning of life and only becomes clearer as life progresses. Frequently the incidents of our lives make more sense to us when we look back on them with the advantage of greater experience.

The child is father of the man, but God is Father of the child because He makes the plans for each of us. What we see more clearly when we look back at our own early experiences is God's plan unfolding step by step, leading us to our present state of being.

As you read this book, please remember that Ralph Di-Orio is not the Gift and the Gift is not Ralph DiOrio. God is the Gift. Ralph DiOrio is merely the man beneath the Gift.

One

PRIVILEGED
HERITAGE

I was born in Providence, Rhode Island, on July 19, 1930. At that time my parents, Ralph and Molly DiOrio, were living in the first-floor apartment of a house owned by my mother's parents, who lived above us on the second floor with my aunts and uncles.

My mother's parents, particularly her father, exerted a very strong influence on my life. The immigrant journey they were destined to make led to my being born in Providence (I've always believed it to be a very auspicious name).

My grandfather, Benedetto Pazienza, met and married my grandmother, Crocifissa Flori, in Rome, Italy. The Floris were a staunchly religious family. Several of my grandmother's brothers and cousins were priests, and there were at least half a dozen nuns in the family. One of my grandmother's uncles, in fact, was named to be a Cardinal, but he died before he was officially invested. Viewed in this light, my own priesthood can easily be seen as part of my family tradition.

My grandparents had already begun to raise a family when Grandpa, whom I always called Nonno Betto (*nonno* is Italian for grandpa, and Betto is the affectionate diminutive for Benedetto), made his first trip to America in search of a better life for himself and his family.

But strangely enough, in order to help his wife and children, he had to leave them first. Like many other men of his period, Nonno Betto had to strike out for the New World alone to find work, set up a home, and send back the passage money so his family could join him. He belonged to that immigrant generation which has been called The Uprooted because the harsh economic prospects of their times tore them loose from their native lands and led them to try their chances in the New World. It is hard for us to imagine now how frightening a challenge that must have been.

Like most of his fellow immigrants, who came from all the nations of Europe, Nonno Betto derived from honest, hardworking stock. Some immigrant men fell ill and died, some deserted their families, but I believe the great majority, like Nonno Betto, worked hard, scrimped, and saved their pennies so they could send for their families.

When Grandpa came to America the first time, he found work in Chicago. It was hard work and the pay was meager, but Grandpa scrimped and managed to save some money each week. After a year or two, he returned to Italy to fetch his wife and children, one of whom was my mother; she was two years old when she came to America.

Upon his return to America, Grandpa decided to settle down with his family in Providence, Rhode Island. He got a job, and as soon as he was able, he bought a house and set about the Old World task of creating a home, a *casa* for his growing family. One of the first things he did, just like many other Italian immigrants I've known, was to transform his backyard into an Italian garden which could provide delicious things to eat and beautiful things to see. Among other delights, he planted grape vines and plum trees. Later on, when I was a small boy, I often sat in the shade of one of those plum trees and listened to my grandpa's wonderful stories. He could be a marvelous and eloquent storyteller, especially when my grandma was not around to interrupt him. And on other occasions, I helped Nonno Betto make wine from the grapes he grew himself. But I'm jumping ahead of the story.

My father was born in Providence, and he was a first generation American. His family was also from Italy; Naples, to be exact. The DiOrios were good, hardworking, honest people, but they were not, I think, deeply religious. They were less spiritual and more worldly than my mother's family, though they were not more successful materially. In fact, they struggled to overcome poverty. Making ends meet was always a problem. The conditions of their lives caused them to view the world in a practical, pragmatic way. No, my father's people were not particularly religious, but they were respectful of the Church.

When Dad first met Mom, she was working in an ice cream parlor. It was there that he began to court her. One of the ways he got her attention was by teasing her. After work, he'd wait for her. She pretended to be annoyed by his persistence and would start walking home, but I think she walked just fast enough to be caught, for caught she was.

Dad met Mom's parents and in his insistent way told them if they did not grant him her hand in marriage with their blessings, he would steal her away and marry her just the same. As was often the case, my father prevailed. Nonno Betto and Nonna Crocifissa acquiesced, and Ralph DiOrio married Ismalia Pazienza. Dad was seventeen, Mom nineteen.

Nonno Betto made room for the new couple in his first-floor apartment, and they settled in to start their own family. A year later God blessed them with their first child. He was a boy. There was much joy in the family, but the process of selecting a suitable name for the small newcomer soon developed into an argument between the grandfathers, Nonno Betto and Nonno Luigi. Then my father solved the problem and settled the issue once and for all. As our family tradition has it, my dad cleared his throat and roared above the din of the squabble, "He will be called after me— Ralph!" There was no room for discussion. My father carried the day, and that's how I came to be named Ralph, which is the Americanized version of the Italian name Rafaelo.

The choice of my name seemed to have come about by chance. If my grandfathers could have reached an agreement, I probably would have been named after some great uncle or other family notable from the past. But they argued, my father grew impatient, and he shared his name with me. Little did he know, at that time, that I also shared the name with one of Mom's uncles, Padre Rafaelo, a priest. Nor was my father truly aware that the name also belonged to the angel Raphael and that in its original Hebrew and Old Testament meaning the name means "medicine of God" or "healer."

I have always felt that my childhood was special, that it was privileged in ways that seem to have grown rare today. In those days of the Great Depression, we never had much money, though we always seemed to have the things we needed. But what we had in abundance were the truly important things that money cannot buy. Most of all, we had our large extended family which included my parents, grandparents, aunts, uncles, and cousins. Our family provided a world full of warmth, love, and mutual support. I was nourished in all the important ways—physical, emotional, social, and spiritual.

My early family life must have been very much like family life had been in the old country. Our whole neighborhood, for that matter, was made up of immigrants. Most of us were Italian, but there was a healthy admixture of Irish families, along with some families from other European countries. In the great American tradition, our neighborhood was a melting pot in which foreign-born immigrants and their native-born children were all going about the business of becoming Americans.

In retrospect I can see my old neighborhood in a sociological and historical perspective, but when I was a child I *experienced* it, lived it, and tasted it, within the nourishing context of my family. By "family" I mean two things: both the individual unit of my mother, my father, and me, and the larger extended family presided over by Nonno Betto.

Next to my parents, Nonno Betto was the most important person in my childhood years. He was a remarkable man. So remarkable, in fact, that even now when I think about him—may his soul rest in peace—I still discover new depths to his character. And that's the word that sums him up best —Nonno Betto was a man of great *character*. He effortlessly combined strength and tenderness; practical and spiritual values; and authority and humor. All in all, Nonno Betto was the perfect model of a traditional family patriarch.

I imagine every boy must find his grandfather interesting, but I don't think there could ever be a grandfather who was *more* compelling or captivating than Nonno Betto. Even today I can still see Nonno Betto sitting at the breakfast table. He got up at five o'clock every morning, and he had to have his veal made with wine and vinegar with a lot of red-hot pepper on top. And then he would have his glass of wine with an egg broken into it. He ate very slowly and savored his food. When you watched Nonno Betto eat, you could almost taste the luscious food, and you'd want to sit down and talk with him and eat with him. When he finished eating he'd walk to work, three miles, and work all day at a factory in Providence. Then he'd walk back the three miles to the house. His life-style must have agreed with him— Nonno Betto lived to be ninety-six.

As with most Italian families, the preparation and the eating of meals was very important in our household. Some of my fondest childhood memories center around mealtimes. Every evening, when all the adults had returned from their jobs, the whole family would gather around the dinner table —there were always at least a dozen of us. Nonna Crocifissa, my aunts, and my mother would carry bowls and platters heaped with food to the table until it seemed there would be no room left.

Almost all of the food we ate was homemade, and I don't mean a cake made from a cake mix bought at the supermarket or string beans from the frozen food chest. Grandma and her daughters, whom she'd taught to cook, made things like *polenta* (a kind of corn mush), various *sugos* (sauces), pickled vegetables, raviolis, bread, cakes, pastries, and sometimes Grandma made her own pasta.

When the table was heaped with food, we all sat down.

Nonno Betto, of course, sat at the head of the table. Everything and everyone was ready, but no one ate or even spoke until Grandpa said a grace over the food. Then Grandma would begin to serve him. As soon as he was satisfied that his wife was serving him, he'd say, "Give me, I'll do it myself." After he filled his plate with pasta, he called for *vino*. As soon as Grandma filled his glass with his own homemade wine, Nonno Betto would look around the table, a twinkle in his eye, and say, "*Che sucessa qui? Non si parla quando si mangia?* What is this? Doesn't anyone speak at table?" And at that moment, everyone started to talk at once to tell what their day had been like. I was the youngest at the table and didn't say very much, but I wished I had more ears so I could hear every one of the overlapping conversations.

Grandpa was king at the head of the table, and I was his little "Junior." He allowed me to sit next to him at his left side. As everyone talked and shared the homemade food, Nonno Betto would wink his eye at me, puff up his flowing mustache, and say, "*Vino?*"

I would be instantly elated at the thought that Nonno Betto and I would share a drink of his homemade *vino*. He made the wine downstairs in the cellar with the grapes he'd picked from his own vines. Sometimes I helped him. We'd put on rubber boots and trample on the grapes in big tubs. Then he'd pour the juice into large wooden vats, where it would sit until it turned to wine.

Because I'd helped him make the wine, I felt a special thrill when he invited me to drink some with him at the dinner table in front of the whole family. It was no ordinary event. First Nonno Betto carefully poured my wine; then he showed me how to enjoy a good homemade wine in the proper Italian style. He'd hand me the glass, saying, "*Piano, piano.* Slowly, slowly." He wanted me to sip it slowly so I could savor the taste and aroma. When I did as he asked, his face beamed and he shouted, "*Bravissimo!*"

When my lips were reddened with the wine, I continued my meal. I was well satisfied because my grandfather had given me a lesson on how a man should conduct himself, even with a glass of homemade wine.

I got along well with all my aunts and uncles—Evelyn, Rose, Ralph, Joe—but my favorite was my Uncle Angelo— God rest his soul. I loved my Uncle Angelo; there was something special about him. He had great energy and high spirits, and he was always doing something exciting and interesting.

Uncle Angelo was a prizefighter. He boxed professionally under the name Kid Island. He was also a dancer. And he played the harmonica—I'd listen as long as he would play and always wanted him to play more. Uncle Angelo loved me too. When I did something wrong and my mother intended to punish me, Uncle Angelo would intercede and try to prevent the punishment, whether I deserved it or not. But my mother didn't get angry at him—at least not truly angry—because she also loved him especially.

I don't think anyone could get truly angry at Uncle Angelo, though he did some irresponsible things and certainly was the wildest member of the family. Nonno Betto used to worry about him; he was afraid Angelo would never settle down to a stable life. But even Nonno Betto could not be stern with Uncle Angelo, and there was invariably a twinkle in his eye when he shook his finger at Angelo over the dinner table and shouted, "*Vagabondo!* What will become of you?"

Uncle Angelo, my high-spirited, irresistible Uncle Angelo, died in his early thirties of spinal meningitis. His body was laid out in the dining room. I sat up all night watching my uncle's body. I thought, God takes those whom He loves the best. It was my first experience seeing death, and I wondered if death was the ultimate end, or if there was something beyond.

I spent many hours at Nonno Betto's side because I loved to be near him. Later on, I understood he kept me close so he could instruct me. He would take me to his toolshed— he built it himself—and patiently show me how to use each of the tools, one by one. He taught me to respect tools and take care of them. He made me understand that a tool, like anything else, for that matter, could be used for good or for evil.

Grandpa often spoke to me about the importance of doing a job well, of doing a task or a chore the way it should be done. Aside from the inner satisfaction of doing something right, a job well done brings the best, most lasting result. As if to demonstrate his precept that honest labor bears honest fruits, Grandpa introduced me to the art of caring for grapevines. It is a long, slow process. Vines have to be tended and pruned carefully for several years before they are ready to bear a crop. But Grandpa went about the process of tending his vines with calm good humor. He was confident that if he did things in the right way, and if the Lord was willing, his vines would bear a rich bounty. Needless to say, Grandpa's grape crops grew lush, and there was always much homemade *vino* in his cellar.

When Grandpa did carpentry work or took care of his garden, I especially liked to watch his hands. Though he'd lost a couple of fingers in an accident at the factory where he worked, his hands were still marvelous. They seemed capable of creating anything.

Like his character, Nonno Betto's hands were a blend of strength and gentleness. Also, they were beautifully expressive.

Often we sat in the garden, beneath the shade of one of his plum trees, while he told me stories about his life and talked to me of his beliefs. As he spoke, his hands danced in the air as if to coax his words or help them along.

Nonno Betto was a God-loving, churchgoing man who believed in the old-time traditional religion. He frequently spoke to me of God and church. His earnest, homespun stories and observations about religion fired my young imagination. When he paused, I'd cry out, "*Piu, Nonno, piu, molto di piu!* Tell me more, Grandpa!"

When I grew older, I realized that Grandpa had passed

his devout belief in traditional Catholicism on to me, and I had taken it deeply to heart.

Grandpa was also a religious mentor to me in another way. The earliest memory I have of a religious experience in church is of a day when Grandpa took me to church with him, though that incident is not my first recollection of church.

My earliest childhood memory of church goes back to the time when I was four or five years old, and my father took me to church. As I've said, my father was not an exceptionally religious man, but he was respectful. In my memory of this incident, Dad held my hand as we walked along. I can still recall what I wore that day—a little white suit with short pants, high white stockings, and white shoes. I wore a small white cap on my head. Hand in hand, father and son, my dad and I walked to church.

That walk to church is very clear in my memory, but I have no such clear recollection of what happened in the church on that particular day. I do have a vivid memory, however, of what happened after church. My father took me to a drugstore and bought me a double-dip ice cream cone—one scoop chocolate and the other vanilla. And he also had my photograph taken. In those days, professional photographers always seemed to be around, willing to take your portrait for a few cents. The photographer in the drugstore that day used a bulky camera on a wooden tripod, and the light came from old-fashioned flash powder.

Perhaps I remember the double-dip ice cream cone and the photograph so clearly because they were somewhat unusual. I grew up in the Great Depression, when we couldn't afford many luxuries. Times were difficult for families all over the country. Both my parents had to work and work hard to earn a living. My father was a stonecutter, and my mother worked as a lacquer sprayer in a factory. In those days my parents had to get up at five o'clock in the morning to get ready for work. When I was a small boy, I always got up with them. I have retained the habit of rising early to this day.

When I set my mind to it, I can still see myself sitting on the floor in front of the kitchen stove—it was a coal burner, and it threw enough heat to warm a couple of rooms—putting on my long stockings, my corduroy knickers, and my shoes. While I got dressed, I could smell the delicious aromas filling the kitchen. By the time I tied my shoes and sat down at the table, my mother had laid out a big breakfast. Father only had toast and coffee, but I had orange juice, pancakes or oatmeal, and lots of hot Ovaltine. After breakfast, my mother and father walked me to the nursery school which was staffed by Catholic Sisters of the Apostolate, or the Pallatine Sisters, as they were also known.

The nursery school day began at seven o'clock in the morning and didn't end until four or five o'clock in the afternoon when my mother or father came to pick me up. I attended that nursery school from the age of three to the age of seven, but the days never seemed long because I had the nuns, the wonderful Pallatine Sisters.

Those Sisters seemed to treat me with a special warmth and love, as if they were looking beyond the little boy they were taking care of, as if they could already see the role that God had chosen for me to play.

In retrospect, I can see now that perhaps I was a somewhat unusual child. In fact, many people who knew me, even when I was only a small boy, always seemed to make prophecies about me. They called me "the nice little boy" and even "the little holy one." In Italian, they called me "*santino*." A few years later the older men of the neighborhood, who witnessed me going to serve daily mass and evening benediction, would smilingly remark, "*Ecco un altro prete*. Here is another priest." Since I wasn't sure of their intentions, I acted courteously and responded, "*Buon giorno, Signori*," or "*Buona serra*"; then I would continue on my way to church.

The Pallatine Sisters, I believe, also saw a priest in me, at least the makings of a priest, and they were very gentle in the ways they directed me. They always extended a hand of guidance, directing me toward the possibility of becoming a minister of God.

Much later, during my seminary years, these godly women, especially Mother Assunta, Sister Candida, Sister Maximillian, and Sister Mary Pia, became even closer to me. Because they understood how difficult and arduous the seminary life was, they used to write encouraging letters which gave me moral and spiritual support. In that extremely important period of my life, these Sisters became as God's temporary auxiliary Grace, encouraging me with their own spiritual insights.

I have never forgotten those inspiring and uplifting letters or the Sisters who wrote them. Their devotion and encouragement motivated me to continue on in the arduous calling that the Lord had given to me. I was truly fortunate to have had those Sisters taking care of me when I was a small child in their nursery school because they were extraordinary women who had much to offer. By virtue of my parents' influence over me, and by my natural gifts from God, I was well disposed toward receiving what these Sisters gave.

✣

One Holy Thursday, when I was about five years old, Nonno Betto took me to the lower church of St. Bartholomew's Parish, the home parish in which my parents had been married. That day I had my first religious experience in a church.

Nonno Betto and I sat at the back of the church. Those were the days of the old liturgy, and after the Holy Thursday services were concluded, I saw a statue of the body of Christ which portrayed Him as if in the tomb—the Corpus Christi. He seemed to rest on a bed of flowers, mostly lilies, and their sweet aroma rose up and spread through the church. I was old enough to understand that I was looking at a statue, but I was deeply impressed. I felt that I wanted to do something for Him. I can still see myself, a little boy in the soft light of the church, wishing I could have helped that Man who died.

When I asked, "Nonno Betto, what does all this mean?" Grandpa answered softly, "My child, this is the day on which the King's Son died for us."

I was at a most impressionable age, and I received a lasting impression. When Nonno Betto took me out of the church, the image of the Corpus of Christ resting amid the sweet-smelling lilies was fixed in my mind. Perhaps it was just the imaginings of a small boy, but maybe God was at work planting this first seed in me.

About the same time, I had another memorable experience in church. Some of my cousins came over one Sunday morning and asked me if I'd like to go to church with them. They took me to the children's mass. The church was packed, and I sat in the back. I couldn't see anything except the heads of hundreds of children.

All I could hear was the strident voice of a woman leading us in prayer, and I didn't like her voice. And then there was a priest, and I didn't like the priest's voice either because he was harsh, or at least that's how his voice sounded to me at that moment. And he said, "If you don't do this or don't do that, you will go to hell. And if you don't do this today, we will punish you." And in my five- or six-year-old mind I thought, "Gee, this is supposed to be the house of God." My idea of God was that He would be somebody you loved and Who loved us, and I thought if I was ever a priest, I would want people to come to church to see that God was love.

❖

When I was seven years old, we moved away from Providence. In search of better work, Dad moved Mom and me to Cranston, Rhode Island. The distance between Providence and Cranston does not seem very great if you look on a map, but it was far enough to take me away from daily contact with the world of Nonno Betto. Thus ended one phase of my life. Another was to begin almost immediately, and it was signaled by one of the great events in my life: my first Holy Communion.

I was seven years old when I made my First Communion. I was dressed in a blue suit which had knickers instead of long pants. I wore a white shirt and a white tie and I had a white ribbon for the First Communion. It was the first time I received Jesus in the Blessed Sacrament, and I took Jesus into my heart. All I could think was, "Jesus, I love You. Stay with me. Don't let me leave You." We were very emotional, and my mother was crying.

After my First Communion, I went to confession regularly. My mother and I availed ourselves of weekly confession. The weekly confessions did not come about because I was guilty of sins, but rather my mother brought me so I could receive Sacramental Grace and thus enrich the spiritual character of my soul. I followed my mother's holy example.

When I was seven years old, I also started Catholic parochial school at St. Anthony's, but the costs were difficult to meet. The Depression was not yet over, and my parents were having difficulties making ends meet. I have never forgotten the crushing poverty of the Depression. Sometimes Dad and Mom were both out of work. One afternoon my father took me with him to do an errand. He held my hand, and we went to a place that looked like a relief office, though I don't know what it was exactly. Nevertheless, I've never forgotten that we were there to pick up some food. I have also never forgotten that my father had to sign some papers before he could get a couple of cans of tuna fish so we would have enough food to eat at home. In such difficult times, my parents just couldn't afford the Catholic education, so they took me out of St. Anthony's and enrolled me in public school. It was the Ralph Street School.

Of all my public school teachers, I have always remembered Miss Lemon the best. She was so young and beautiful that we all fell in love with her. One day, while we were sitting on small stools in a circle for our reading lesson, I had a small accident. I was holding my book open on my lap. When my turn came to read, my knee moved and the book slipped. I grabbed for it and accidentally ripped a small triangle from the corner of a page.

Miss Lemon burst into a fury, shouting that I had damaged public school property. At that moment she destroyed my little boy's love for her. I was perplexed because I'd always been well behaved, and I couldn't understand why she suddenly acted like a witch. I can still see that classroom and hear her voice.

"You go home this minute," Miss Lemon shouted, "and tell your mother that you ripped your book!"

I was frightened, but I managed to say, "But I didn't rip it. It was an accident."

I knew I hadn't done anything wrong, anything for which I should be sent home to tell my mother. But I was afraid to be naughty. When I went home, I was scared stiff. I was only a little seven-year-old, and I was tense, nervous, and frightened.

I waited for my mother to come home from work. It seemed like a very long time. When I finally saw her walking down the street with several other women, women who also worked in the factory, I wondered how on earth I was going to tell my mother that she had to pay thirty-five cents for a book I accidentally ripped. When the moment came, I couldn't bring myself to tell her.

The next morning at school, Miss Lemon grabbed hold of me as soon as I walked into the classroom. "Did you tell your mother? Did you bring the money?"

"Oh, no," I said, "I don't have the money."

"Well, did you tell your mother?"

At that moment I told my first lie, or at least the first one that I remember. I said in a halting voice, "Yes, I told my mother."

"Well, what did your mother say?"

I hadn't planned that far ahead; it never occurred to me

that Miss Lemon might ask what my mother had said, so I hadn't prepared an answer. But I had to answer Miss Lemon's question. I blurted out, "My mother said if I do it again to let her know."

The absurdity of my answer seemed to stun Miss Lemon.

There was a long silence. Miss Lemon seemed flabbergasted, but she didn't say a word. She just dropped the subject, and that was the end of it. Nothing ever happened.

I felt betrayed by the way Miss Lemon suddenly turned on me. Small children frequently form deep attachments to a teacher. When that happens, the teacher has a responsibility to be considerate and not hurt the child.

Of course, teachers are only human. Perhaps Miss Lemon was having a bad day. And who can tell what kind of terrible problems she was facing in her private life outside of school? But I believe that teachers and others who occupy positions of authority and leadership must try harder. They must make that extra effort, even if it's very difficult, to return the love and admiration of their students with love and admiration of their own.

❖

The routine and style of our family life in Cranston were different than they had been in Providence. The main difference, as I see it now, was the absence of our extended family. Now it was just the three of us—Mom, Dad, and I. In this sense, we lived more in the American style of each individual unit of the entire family going its own way. The three of us grew even closer, but we missed the warmth and support of our relatives and our old neighborhood.

Shortly after we moved to Cranston, I was deprived of my mother for the first time in my life. It was a temporary loss, to be sure, but it stamped a deep impression on my eight-year-old psyche. This incident came about when my mother fell ill. She took to her bed, and what seemed to be a very long time passed by, but she did not get better. I was worried about my mother and I prayed for her, but I was too young actually to understand what was going on.

Late one afternoon an ambulance pulled up in front of our house, and two attendants jumped out. They pulled a stretcher out of the ambulance and ran up the stairs. As I had no idea that an ambulance would be coming, the sudden arrival of the attendants, who burst right into our apartment without even knocking, surprised and frightened me. They quickly lifted my mother off the bed, placed her on the stretcher, carried her down to the ambulance, and put her in.

The whole scene unfolded as quickly as I have described it. The attendants hardly said a word as they went about their business. My father was almost speechless too. He was grief-stricken. His face was white, and he never took his eyes off my mother as the attendants carried her out. He followed behind them. When they slid her into the ambulance, he too got in. One of the attendants slammed the rear door, and the ambulance roared off down the street.

Suddenly I was alone. It was late in the afternoon. Darkness had begun to fall. Through the dusk I watched the red lights of the ambulance speed down the road carrying my mother and father away from me. The red lights got smaller, then abruptly disappeared when the ambulance turned a corner. I burst into tears. All I could do was run back into the house. I rushed up the stairs and ran to the small altar my mother had built. I threw myself down and knelt before the crucifix. "Jesus," I cried, "save my mother! Please bring her back to me!" I prayed to God to send His Healing Grace. "Make my mother better, Jesus, I beg of You to heal her!" It was the first time in my life that I prayed for someone to be healed.

It was fitting and appropriate that my mother should have been the first person for whose healing I directly and consciously prayed. It was also meaningful and significant, for this event which occurred when I was eight years old foreshadowed an event which took place thirty-seven years later and which marked another major breakthrough in my life.

One day in 1976 I drove from St. John's parish in Worcester, Massachusetts, where I was assigned, down to Providence,

Rhode Island, to visit my mother. I knew she was not feeling well, but I was not prepared to find her as ill as she was. I was deeply concerned for her health, but instead of my usual optimism, I grew momentarily frustrated by the feeling of helplessness that came over me.

My mother drew me out of my moment of despair by asking me to pray over her. I hesitated at first, but under her guidance I placed my hands on her head and once again prayed for her healing. Nothing happened, or at least nothing I was aware of. I drove back to Worcester, still deeply concerned about my mother's health.

Later that evening when I phoned my mother to see how she was, she told me that after I left she'd felt dizzy for about an hour. She said she'd experienced waves of heat passing through her body and now felt healed, almost as if she'd never been ill. I was delighted, greatly relieved that she seemed better, though I made no conscious connection between the fact of my having prayed over her and the fact that she now felt healed. I could not yet see that God was beginning to work His power through me and use me as His channel. But I didn't have long to wait.

My mother's healing occurred on May 4, 1976. Five days later, on May 9, during a visit to a charismatic service at St. Patrick's Church in Cambridge, Massachusetts, I openly broke out with God's Gift of Healing. On that day God revealed one more step in His plan to use me as a channel for transmitting His Heavenly Grace. It was the same plan which He had foreshadowed that dark afternoon when the ambulance carried my mother away, and I ran back to my house and prayed for her healing.

On that dark afternoon I was alone in our apartment. In his great anxiety over my mother, my father accompanied her to the hospital without having made any arrangements for me. But our next-door neighbors, a generous German family, kept an eye on me. They knew I was alone, and their children came over and took me back to their house for supper. They made me feel very comfortable, and I stayed with them until my father got home.

When he returned, my father brought the good news that my mother's crisis had passed. Though she would have to spend some more time in the hospital recuperating, my mother was going to get better. My prayer for her healing had been answered.

While my mother was in the hospital, my father continued to work, and I continued to attend school. I was only eight years old and somewhat on my own, but it hardly bothered me. When Mom was healthy, the usual arrangement was for both her and Dad to work, anyway, so I was used to being alone.

All of my life I've been a self-contained, self-sufficient kind of person, so I was not lonely when I was alone. The distinction between being alone and being lonely is a very important one, though many people fail to understand it. I was not lonely for the simple reason that I enjoyed my own company. I still do. I love people—all people—it is one of the reasons that I am a priest. But there are times, particularly in the morning, when I must be alone with my own thoughts and my own self.

I've always felt sorry for people who seem unable to be alone with themselves, even for a few minutes. How sad it is —perhaps even tragic—when people must turn on their radios or TVs as soon as they wake up in the morning, as if they are afraid to experience an empty moment in which they will have to face themselves.

It is my belief that each of us should try to begin the day with a few moments of quiet contemplation so we can get in touch with ourselves and with our God. In this way, we also become better prepared to be in touch with and help each other.

❖

Until the age of thirteen I was an only child. Our house was quiet for long stretches of time, just right for the kinds of boyhood pursuits which interested me. One of my favorite pastimes was listening to the radio while drawing pictures of what I imagined the radio characters looked like. The programs I liked best included "Jack Armstrong," "Let's Pretend," "Hop Harrington," and "Don Winslow of the Navy."

The radio programs stimulated my imagination and helped to develop my own God-given, natural gift for storytelling. My drawings were also an expression of a natural gift—I have always had some talent and inclination toward the visual arts. My artistic abilities, I believe, were inherited from my father who used to create his own beautiful and original designs for gravestones. Later, with his mallet and chisels, he carved his designs into the stones.

My father was a skilled craftsman in several other areas. He was an excellent carpenter and an able, self-taught mechanic. He always seemed able to figure out how a broken machine was supposed to work and fix it. For a time he used to go around and fix oil burners in people's houses. I was twelve or thirteen then, and often I'd go with him, particularly on night calls, and watch over his tools.

Like most boys, I imitated the things I saw my father do—and also the things I'd seen Nonno Betto do. I played baseball and war games and did the things other boys did, but the hobbies and activities I enjoyed most involved making things in emulation of my father and grandfather.

During my childhood years, I did many carpentry projects, but I especially remember the model airplanes I built. They were the old kind, made of thin strips of balsa wood and covered with a special kind of tissue paper. I used to fly my models in a big field near our house. It was a marvelous feeling to fly a model you had patiently built up with your own hands and watch it curve through the air like a racing bird. When you started to build such a model, all you had was a pile of supplies—balsa wood, common pins, glue, tissue paper, and a blueprint. To the inexperienced eye, it would never have looked possible that these things could be put together in such a way that they would actually fly. But I was un-daunted; even as a child I loved a challenge.

My interest in arts and crafts was strong and obvious. Some of my public school teachers observed it and began to en-courage me. They complimented my work, offered advice, and made suggestions about possible careers in design, com-mercial art, or drafting.

I appreciated this attention from my teachers. It increased my self-confidence and led me to think more seriously about the future. Looking back on my life from the vantage point of today, I see that my interest in art was so genuine that I might very well have chosen an artistic career if I hadn't entered the seminary.

As I mentioned earlier, I believe I inherited my artistic inclinations from my father. He was extremely proud of my work and always had a word of praise or encouragement for one of my paintings, drawings, or models.

When I was old enough for my future to be a topic of dis-cussion at home, my father revealed his dream. He wanted me to join him in our own "father-and-son" business, design-ing and carving all types of stonework. It was a beautiful dream, but it was not to be. Other forces—more powerful forces—were acting on my life and directing it toward an-other goal.

Every child receives elements of personality and ability from both parents, though the contributions may not be of equal size or importance. Art and a natural appreciation of beauty were my father's bequests. From my mother I re-ceived spirituality, compassion, and a desire to heal.

My mother is a very compassionate woman, especially toward the sick and the suffering. She too has been granted a healing gift, and when I was young it seemed she was always going to help a neighbor or relative who was ill. She was the one they asked for.

Her compassion extended to all God's creatures. She al-ways encouraged me to help the sick or wounded animals which I frequently brought home. One cold winter day I found a wounded sparrow in the snow. I couldn't tell if it was alive or dead. I cupped it in my hands to keep it warm and ran home. The little bird thawed out in our warm kitchen. When she got home, my mother said I could take care of it. And so I nursed the sparrow back to health. When it was ready, I opened the window. The sparrow hopped out onto the window ledge, cocked its head back at me once, and flew away.

This predisposition toward healing the sick caused me to give some thought to a career in medicine. I was only a child, but what little I knew about psychiatry seemed immensely worthwhile to me. Healing people's emotional problems and sufferings seemed like a wonderful thing to do for them. So along with my thoughts about art, I entertained thoughts of becoming a doctor, perhaps a psychiatrist.

These dreams were somewhat unrealistic. My parents were hardworking people who sometimes had trouble making ends meet. Without scholarships or other financial aid, they never could have afforded to put me through medical school. But in reality, my thoughts about careers in art or medicine were only speculations and exercises. The path of my life had already been unalterably turned in God's direction and toward the Church.

My mother, who has always been an especially devout woman, went to church frequently. Usually she took me with her. This was how and when I first met Father Ulderico Piccolo, a young priest who had just come to our parish directly from Italy. He was an old-world Italian with a manner and style that was very familiar. He reminded me of the old neighborhood in Providence, though he didn't remind me of any particular person. I liked him immediately, but none of us realized at the time what a profound and lasting influence Father Piccolo was to have on my life.

One of my first memories of Father Piccolo is of the time I was in the confession box and he asked me if I'd like to be an altar boy. This invitation to be part of the holy service thrilled me. It seemed to be the thing I'd been waiting for; I got so excited I could hardly believe my ears. "Father, you mean to serve the mass?" I asked in amazement. "Yes, Ralph," he answered in Italian, "that's exactly what I mean—to serve the mass." I was elated, but I blurted out my fear: "Father, I don't know if I can learn the Latin!" In those days of the Latin liturgy, altar boys had to know certain parts of the mass in Latin. Father Piccolo laughed and in his good-natured Italian way assured me that I could do it.

Later, I attended a meeting with the other youngsters who had been chosen to be altar boys. We each received a copy of the altar boy's book which we had to study. Then we began the classes in which nuns taught us the things we had to know to perform our new roles in the church ritual.

My parents, particularly my mother, were elated with my selection. They encouraged me in whatever ways they could. And one of my public school teachers, Miss Fowler, went out of her way to assist me. As it turned out, Miss Fowler had seen my inclination toward a religious vocation from the very beginning. When she heard that I was in training, she gave me time during class to study my altar boy's book. She even helped me with the Latin.

To this day I remain grateful to Miss Fowler for her kindness and concern. Nevertheless, just as I had feared, I found the Latin very difficult. I thought I'd never learn it. Then I became downhearted and felt I'd fallen so far behind the others that I'd never be able to catch up. With feelings of shame and failure, I stopped going to the altar boys' lessons without explaining anything to anyone except my mother.

A few days later, while my mother was making her confession and I was waiting to make mine, Father Piccolo asked her why I'd stopped going to the lessons. She told him about the trouble I'd been having with the Latin. "Is that so?" he asked and came right out of the confessional. He walked over to me. "Ralph, I'd like to take you under my wing and teach you the Latin myself. Would you like that?"

I was overwhelmed. His offer was out of the ordinary, and I felt I could not refuse it. I still worried about the Latin, but I thought about it for a minute and came to the immediate conclusion that if anyone I personally knew could help me learn the Latin, it was Father Piccolo. So I looked up at him and answered, "Yes, Father, I would like that very much."

For the next few months, my daily schedule was full. Every day after public school classes were over, I had to walk the four miles to church quickly in order to get there in time for my lesson with Father Piccolo. But the effort was worthwhile. Father was kind to me, and very patient in his lessons. In and around the Latin lessons, he wove a pattern of stories which introduced me to various aspects of the priestly life. In his own friendly way, Father Piccolo drew forth my vocation for the priesthood.

I was an altar boy for eight years. As time passed, I began to realize that I was feeling more and more at home in church. I liked school and I liked my home life, but there was something about being at the church, in God's house among His priests, that seemed deeply natural to me. I was aware of this feeling, but I didn't often think of it, nor did I try to give it a definite shape by putting it into words.

About this time, there was a kind of miracle in our house. When my mother had been dangerously ill when I was a small boy, her doctors told her she could not possibly have any more children. But five years later, she became pregnant. In December 1943, when I was thirteen, my brother Louis was born.

For the next year or so, Mom was not herself. It took her a long time to regain her strength. During that period, I assumed a lot of household and baby-care chores.

In the morning, I got up at five o'clock and helped Dad make coffee. When he left for work, I jumped on my scooter and rolled down the hill to church in time to serve seven o'clock mass. When I returned home, Mom would some-times still be in bed, unless she was feeling particularly strong. I'd make and serve her breakfast, eat my own, then roll up my sleeves and wash little Louis' dirty diapers.

In those days, home washing machines were rare, we couldn't afford a diaper service, and disposable diapers didn't exist yet. When you had dirty diapers you washed them by hand. Now that I recall it, I think everyone should wash a diaper sometime in their life. It puts you in touch with humility and the everlasting glory of God's great creation—human life.

After the diapers were done, I'd take the three-mile walk to school. School was enjoyable. I was interested in my classes and felt I was learning something. The teachers were somewhat strict but, for the most part, fair with the students. Many of the teachers seemed to like me. One or two of them took an interest in my future and discussed possible careers with me.

I listened to everyone, but in those days the man I ad-mired the most was Father Piccolo. I spent as much time with him as I could. He was a holy priest, a good priest, a man who possessed the kind of qualities my mother re-spected and wanted to instill in me. I too respected him very much, and I wanted to emulate him, though I had not yet articulated the thought or the possibility that I might choose to become a priest.

With no definite thought of where my life was heading, I went about my business with energy and interest. My household chores took on added importance, for our family had grown again. A year and a half after Louis was born, my mother had her third and final child, my sister Jude Ann.

I enjoyed my brother and sister. The idea of a large family always appealed to me, and family life certainly was fuller after they came along.

Outside of the house I was concerned with school, my friends, and the Church. My concern with the Church was growing all the time, though I didn't yet perceive the pattern of my life or God's plan for me. Though I didn't know it, my family life, my public school career, and my childhood were about to end.

Two

COME
FOLLOW ME

The rapid events of the spring and summer of 1945 were momentous for the entire world, which was still locked in the deadly struggle of the Second World War. The first of these events was sad. On April 12, President Franklin Delano Roosevelt died. It was a great loss for people everywhere; President Roosevelt was a giant among world leaders. But for Americans, and most particularly for Americans of my generation, it was an irreplaceable loss.

President Roosevelt had first gained office in 1932, at the lowest ebb of the Great Depression. The nation was paralyzed and needed a great leader; FDR turned out to be that man. In my mind, he was a Moses figure who found our nation sick and helped heal it. His innovative New Deal programs brought jobs and paychecks to millions of Americans, my own family and neighbors included.

Roosevelt's death also had a personal meaning for Americans. He had been our president for thirteen years, longer than any man in history. He would have served sixteen years, but he died in the first year of his fourth term. Roosevelt was the only president my generation knew during our whole growing up. His years in office were remarkable, unforgettable. He made a lasting impression on my contemporaries, as much for the things he did as for the long and seemingly endless tenure of his presidency. By comparison, in the last thirteen years we have had four presidents. For whatever reasons, they seem to leave office just as we begin to know something about them. But Roosevelt, during his long incumbency, gave such an appearance of stability and permanence that he became our symbol of the presidency itself. When he died, people cried in the streets, and it seemed an era in our lives died with him.

In May, less than a month after Roosevelt died, Germany surrendered, thus ending the European phase of the Second World War. In June, countries from all over the world signed the charter of the United Nations, whose noble goal was to "save succeeding generations from the scourge of war."

Before August ran its course, the world had entered the nuclear age with the atomic bombing of Hiroshima and Nagasaki. A few days later Japan surrendered, and World War II was finally over.

All of these momentous events happened one after the other in rapid succession. It was probably one of the most memorable four-month periods of the century. But I remember that period for another reason, a more personal one. In the summer of 1945, I made the most important decision of my life.

I decided to become a priest.

During July, I served mass for Father Anthony Cioe, a Franciscan priest who was visiting our parish. He was a childhood friend and classmate of my mother's; they'd grown up together. My mother spoke fondly of him as an irrepressible, impetuous, and warmhearted person. She even forgave his boyish prank of dipping her hair in the inkwell when he'd sat behind her at school.

Father Cioe was an unusual priest. In his mannerisms he affected a gruffness. Sometimes he seemed to act as if he was just one of the fellows, maybe the toughest of the lot. He was a short, compact man who reminded me of Jimmy Cagney; he even talked out of the side of his mouth. But his external behavior did not blind us to his goodness, which shone through like a glow from the Heart of Christ.

His relationship to us altar boys was straightforward. He did not hide behind his cassock or create a formal distance between him and us which would prevent honest communication. He frequently joked with us and established an easygoing air of trust which made it easier for us to talk honestly about issues that may have been embarrassing or sensitive for us.

One day after mass, we altar boys fell to teasing each other about what we'd be when we grew up. Father Cioe joined in. I was one month short of my fifteenth birthday, but I had not yet come to grips with my future in any firm way. All I knew clearly was that I loved the Church and wanted to devote myself to it, but I had no plan. I hung back from forcing the issue in my own mind.

Some of the other altar boys were more direct. When Father asked one of them what he wanted to do when he grew up, the boy quickly responded that his goal was to get married and have a family. When he said that, I laughed.

I laughed to cover my inner feelings. I was unsure of myself. I wished Father Cioe had asked the question of me, or better yet, I wished Father had asked me if I wanted to be a *priest*. The thought had appeared in my mind.

But I was shy and felt inferior. In part, at least, I saw myself as a poor Italian boy whose family lacked the resources which I thought were needed in order to become a priest.

Father Cioe looked at me with his tough-guy grin. "What are you laughing at, Ralph?"

"He wants to get married!" I laughed again. "Ha, ha, ha!"

My laughter, I see now, was my subconscious attempt at getting him to ask me if I wanted to become a priest.

Father Cioe laughed too. "Well, what do you think *you're* going to do?"

At that moment, Father Cioe caused me to respond to a question that had been residing deep within my heart. "Okay," I answered, without really thinking about what I was saying, "I'm going to be a priest." It was the first time I had said those words.

Father responded with gravity and seriousness. He became pensive and asked me quietly, "Do you really want to be a priest?" The way he asked let me know that I *could* become a priest if I *wanted* to.

"Sure," I said. But as I was answering Father's weighty question, I didn't truly know if I meant what I was saying. I was surprised myself at how easily the words had tumbled out of my mouth: "Yes, I do want to be a priest."

At that moment, my first great life decision confronted me. That moment became the fulcrum of my life, the turning point which led to a vocational calling. I was puzzled myself at the force within me which caused me to blurt forth my secret desire. But my heart was full of courage, and I could sense the new force within me beaming out in a confident smile. "Yes," I said again. "Yes. I do want to become a priest."

Father Cioe looked at me with an earnest and thoughtful expression on his face. "Yes, I understand," he said. Then our serious moment ended. The other altar boys resumed their playful conversation. I walked home with the new knowledge that my half-hidden boyhood dreams were seeking fulfillment.

Two weeks later I received a letter from the Franciscan seminary in Lowell, Massachusetts. The letter informed me that I had been accepted as a candidate for the minor seminary. If I replied before September 8—it was already August —I could be enrolled for the new semester.

I was totally flabbergasted, stunned, perplexed. What was I to do? Suddenly the decision-making process which had begun with Father Cioe's question was raised to a new level by the arrival of this letter.

The first thing I did was share the letter with my mother. As always, she was supportive and understanding, but this was a decision I had to make myself. Feeling the need to be alone, I left my house and walked the mile or two to one of my favorite spots, a ledge on the rim of an old stone quarry.

The Ledge, as the spot was locally called, was a place I often visited, sometimes with a friend or two but just as frequently alone. When I went there by myself, I was better able to find communion with the peacefulness and natural beauty of the place. On this occasion, I was alone with the slate-gray cliffs, the green trees, and the endless blue sky.

Undisturbed in the presence of nature, I soon found myself in one of my first true soliloquies directed to God.

God, I asked, are You really calling me to be Your priest? Do I have the qualities in me to fulfill the role of a priest? It this what You want me to be?

While pondering these questions, I wondered what Father Piccolo would think. I'd been close to him for eight years; I was one of his altar boys, and he was also my weekly confessor. During those eight years, he'd had a profound influence on my life. He was an easygoing, optimistic man who reminded me of the priest played by Bing Crosby in the film, *Going My Way,* which Father Piccolo had taken a few of us to see. Who could serve me better as a priestly counselor than Father Piccolo himself?

Father Piccolo was undoubtedly the priest I'd known the longest and the best. He had been in our parish ever since I could remember, and I felt he was *my* priest. I showed him the letter and told him I didn't know what to do.

After he read the letter and thought about it a few minutes, he said, "You've known me for a long time. You seem to like me and respect the kind of priest I am. Well, as you know, I'm a Scalabrini Father. So my advice to you, Ralph, is this—why don't you come to our own Scalabrini seminary? You'll probably feel more comfortable there, more familiar with our way of doing things."

There was definitely truth to what Father Piccolo said. I'd always respected him and esteemed his judgment. But beyond his judgment, the characteristic I deeply appreciated was his apparent spiritual life, his deep union with God. It was that very union with God, that intense spirituality which he shared with his flock, which served as the guiding light for my vocational decision.

But the truth is that I didn't really know what he meant when he said "our" seminary. My knowledge of church organization was so scant that I didn't even know there were different kinds of priests, such as diocesan priests and missionary priests, or that there were different priestly congregations and orders. Father Piccolo was a Scalabrinian priest, but at that time such a distinction meant nothing to me.

After a while, Father Piccolo offered to go to my house and discuss my future with my parents. He was proud of his congregation, the Scalabrinians, and quite naturally he wanted me to join them. But I didn't understand that, either. I was close to him emotionally, so I assumed he'd give advice that was objective and good for me. When I look back on it now, I think he was somewhat unfair to me as far as his counseling and advice were concerned. I was apprehensive about the fact that I'd have to surrender my parents and the closeness of family life. He knew my family, and he should have known that my family needed me nearby, but he just advised me to make the same choice he had made.

When Father Piccolo arrived at our house that afternoon, everything was ready. Coffee, soft drinks, and some home-baked cake were set out. Everything was just so. It was clear that his visit was going to force the issue of my future. It was a scene that I've always remembered clearly.

It was a very hot day, and the windows were open. Father Piccolo sat on a chair. I sat on another chair. And my parents sat on the couch. The three adults talked about my future, but actually Father Piccolo did most of the talking.

As I sat there listening, I realized that I did not want to go to that seminary. It didn't seem to make sense to me. Father Piccolo said it was in Chicago, and I wasn't even sure where Chicago was. He told my parents that I would like it there.

I could tell by the way my father looked that he wasn't happy. He didn't show much externally, but I knew that inside he was in turmoil because he didn't agree with what the priest was advising us to do. My father still had the dream that we would be in business together, that I would make the designs and he would carve the stone. So he was disappointed, but all my father said was I could do what I wanted and that my mother was in charge of me.

I looked at my mother, and she seemed content. Then I looked at Father Piccolo, and he seemed to believe in the advice he was giving us. I realized that I didn't want to go to that seminary, but I submitted. I kept my feelings to my heart and said that I would go to Chicago.

I agreed to go, but in my mind I understood that I was allowing friendship to conquer conviction. To avoid offending Father Piccolo, I said, "Yes, I'll go to the Scalabrinian seminary in Chicago. I'll try."

The manner in which I submitted to Father Piccolo would be repeated over and over in my life, for I did not assert myself; I always deferred my interests and feelings to the interests and needs of others. I didn't want to hurt anybody.

Because I did not know how to say no the future was to hold much pain. I suffered until Bishop Bernard J. Flanagan, the Bishop of Worcester, Massachusetts, accepted me into his diocese and taught me how to say yes and how to say no.

The misgivings and doubts were held inside. But suppressed feelings will eventually break out. My initial doubts about entering the Scalabrinian congregation never disappeared. They plagued me. Eventually they caused me to break with the Scalabrinian congregation, though it took many years for this to come about.

Father Piccolo's mistake with me was based on his human limitations; he couldn't see what would be best for me from my point of view. But perhaps there was no mistake at all; in retrospect, it can honestly be said that my experience with the Scalabrinis, which like most things in life turned out to be a combination of good and bad, was a positive step toward the present healing ministry. In geometry, the theorem states that the shortest distance between two points is a straight line, but God is not a scientist. Who can fathom the ways of Divine Providence?

A few days after his memorable visit, Father Piccolo took me to buy my first black clothes—a black suit and black shoes. Then we informed the public junior high school that I'd be leaving, and on September 5, 1945, I left home with Father Piccolo.

We took the train from Providence to Grand Central Station in New York City. The station was teeming with soldiers, sailors, and marines all trying to get somewhere. The war had been over for less than a month, and there was still a feeling of celebration in the air. The next morning we got on the train to Chicago. It was also full of GIs, but I didn't talk with any of them or even pay much attention to what was going on around me. I was lost in my own thoughts about the new life I was about to enter.

As soon as we arrived in Chicago, we went right from the train station to the rectory in the Holy Guardian Angel parish where several of Father Piccolo's Scalabrini classmates were assigned as parish priests. A group of these priests were having lunch when we arrived, and we accepted their invitation to join them.

The meal quickly developed into a festive occasion celebrating the reunion between Father Piccolo and his old friends. There was much laughter around the table and much high-spirited conversation, all of it in rapid, free-flowing Italian. Like Father Piccolo, his Scalabrinian colleagues were Old World-born.

After dinner, a few of these priests drove Father Piccolo and me out to Sacred Heart Seminary, which was in Melrose Park, Illinois, a few miles outside of Chicago.

Upon our arrival, the rector, who seemed to be an efficient, businesslike administrator, welcomed me. He then summoned the prefect in charge of the students, and I was immediately assigned a room and given my supplies. This was the beginning of my seminary life.

A few days later, Father Piccolo returned to Providence. From that day on, his influence over me waned as I entered more deeply into the world of priestly studies and devotion.

Thus I began the journey on the long road to priesthood—twelve arduous years of intense discipline in prayer and study. The road on which I'd begun to travel would eventually lead to the exalted goal of my consecration as a priest of God, which took place on June 1, 1957, the day on which I was ordained. But in the autumn of 1945, I was just setting out on the road to becoming a Roman Catholic priest in the congregation of the Pious Society of the Missionaries of St. Charles, which is the formal name of the well-known congregation popularly called the Scalabrini Fathers.

The Scalabrini Missionary Congregation was founded in 1887 on the humanitarian principles of benevolence and social service. Its founder, Bishop John Baptist Scalabrini, the bishop of Piacenza in northern Italy, was a man of great social conscience. His ideas and activities were very advanced for his time, which was an era of great social upheaval.

The late 1800s were a time of great unrest, not only in Italy, but in other European countries as well. For millions of people, particularly those of the peasant and working classes, life was very hard. The class system was strong in these countries, and the economic conditions were weak. Jobs were scarce, and wages were low. Opportunities were few and tightly limited where they were available. The paths to fulfillment and success—in many cases even the hard road to survival—seemed blocked on all sides but one. The best solution, the clearest avenue to improvement, pointed in the direction of emigration.

Tens of millions of people left their ancestral villages in the Old World. In a steady stream of humanity, they poured into the growing countries which needed more laborers to build new cities and to work in the mines, on the railroads, and in the factories. The search for better lives led these people to the countries of North and South America and to places such as Australia. But the country which epitomized the land of opportunity was the United States. It was during this period of turmoil, which lasted several decades, that my own grandparents migrated to America.

The newly adopted countries did prove to have more opportunities than the old countries like Italy, but conditions for the immigrants were far from perfect. Wages were low; hours were long. Frequently children, at young ages, had to work if the family was going to survive. Living conditions were crowded, and very often the new immigrants did not speak the language of the new country and did not know its customs and manners, so they tended to be isolated in ethnic neighborhoods. As a result of all these factors, the family life of the immigrants suffered.

In many cases the traditional values, including spirituality, fell away, owing to apathy or lack of leadership, and were not replaced with any other positive values. Just when they needed it most, the immigrants were deprived of the social, emotional, and spiritual support which had always been available in their traditional ancestral villages. Under the intense strain of immigrant life, many people suffered.

As reports of the problems being faced by the new immigrants came back to the Old World, concerned people grew alarmed. Bishop Scalabrini was one of the people who actually did something about the problem. After studying the situation, he concluded that the immigrants needed a very special kind of assistance, a combination of social services and religious leadership which could be administered to the immigrants in their native language.

The immigrant experience of the Italians, to be sure, was not unique. The Greeks, Jews, Poles, Russians, and Slavs, to name some of the others, generally shared the same problems faced by the Italians. But Bishop Scalabrini was himself an Italian. He felt he understood and could do more for the Italian immigrants than for the others. He resolved to organize a group of missionary priests who shared the language, culture, mores, and religious history of the Italian immigrants whose needs they would serve.

Bishop Scalabrini invited the local diocesan priests within his bishopric to take a five-year oath to serve as special missionary priests to Italians living in foreign lands. The diocesan priests responded enthusiastically, and this was the origin of the Scalabrini Fathers.

In the ensuing years, the Scalabrini Fathers performed marvelous, invaluable work in Italian immigrant communities all over the world. They not only supplied the specific type of spiritual leadership needed by their compatriots, but they provided the practical assistance that the immigrants needed to adapt and thrive in their new countries. The enduring success of the Scalabrini Fathers, which continues to this day, amply demonstrates the validity of Bishop Scalabrini's social concerns and the aptness of the missionary congregation he organized. He stands as one of the great social workers in Church history.

From the inception of their congregation, the Scalabrini Fathers have been Italian-born or of Italian descent, such as Italo-Americans like myself. Until recently, their social endeavors were designed exclusively for Italians living in foreign countries. My original contact with the Scalabrini Fathers was by parish affiliation. Because many Italian immigrants lived in Rhode Island, the Scalabrini Fathers staffed five or six parishes in that state. I happened to be born in one of them. So it was by that affiliation that I was led to the Scalabrinian seminary. There had not been any serious career planning, and the implications of becoming a Scalabrinian missionary priest were never made clear to me.

At the age of fifteen, I did not fully understand that the scope of my priesthood would be limited by the very specific goals of the Scalabrinians. I did not perceive that the prescribed functions of Scalabrinian priests, as necessary and laudable as they were, were not compatible with the image of a universal priesthood which I held in my head. The tension between these two models of priesthood plagued me for years. I was vaguely aware of them, but at the time the most important and exciting thing was to begin my studies to become a priest.

Life in the Sacred Heart Seminary was built around an arduous discipline. During my four years as a seminarian, I completed my classical education, which incorporated the equivalent of a high school curriculum; began my priestly education; and entered the life of formal prayer. It was hard work for all of us. Our daily schedule consisted of work, study, and prayer.

On a typical day, we awoke at five-thirty and departed to chapel at six for morning prayer and meditation. At six-thirty we attended mass. Breakfast was served at seven-fifteen, and at a quarter to eight we performed our cleaning duties and attended to other chores. Then morning classes began and lasted until eleven-thirty, when we had a half hour of singing practice. After singing, we returned to the chapel for midday prayers. Afterwards, we went to the refectory for lunch; then the schedule continued in much the same manner until our evening meal was completed. Then we spent several hours studying our lessons. After my nightly prayers, I would get into bed, tired from the work and study but exhilarated by the moments of devotion and prayer.

In my seminary days, the accepted standards for a priestly education were extremely strict, particularly in seminaries like Sacred Heart, which followed a European model of asceticism. Our meals, for example, hardly varied from day to day, and the portions were never too large. All our interests were focused sharply on our priestly studies. The outside world was shut out. We were, in fact, cloistered. We seminarians could not leave the seminary grounds unless we had permission to do so as a group.

As a result of this ascetic system, the worldly sounds which were once so intriguing now became thin and empty to most of us. Our concerns became increasingly spiritual. Nevertheless, the seminary routine lay heavily on us. In this rigorous life we drew our greatest strength from prayer.

Among ourselves, we seminarians discussed the training and education we were receiving and questioned some facets of seminary life. Some students discovered they lacked authentic vocations for becoming Scalabrini priests or, in some cases, for becoming priests at all. These students departed from the seminary.

I also had a problem. However, it didn't concern the authenticity of my priestly vocation. I wanted to be a priest and had no doubt about that. But the unanswered question about the authenticity of a Scalabrinian vocation emerged again as a gnawing doubt. The more I learned about the specific functions of the Scalabrinis, the more I doubted that I was meant to be one of them. I could not seem to abide with an image of a priestly vocation that was limited to being sent out on missions to work with Italian immigrants in Australia or Brazil. My aspiration was a more universal vocation, one in which I could serve all of God's people.

My doubts and questions sought honest discussion and an honest conclusion. This was a period of great suffering in my inner life.

One day I presented myself to the rector for a personal interview. I needed some clarification from him. Doubts about the authenticity of a Scalabrini vocation had begun to cause me anxiety. Did I have the authentic qualities to be a priest? If so, was I being called by God to be a Scalabrini Father?

The rector, Father Pierini, was very responsive. He explained that seminarians frequently were beset with doubts; he himself had known them in his youth. He assured me of my priestly qualities and my Scalabrini vocation. In effect, he tried to assuage all my doubts.

I didn't question Father Pierini's counsel. When I was fifteen or sixteen, I still thought priests had the Word of

God. I listened to his words, and though they didn't match the truth I felt in my heart, I didn't question his advice. I never questioned the advice of priests until I became a priest myself and was able to see that even priests could make some mistakes. Then I saw that the rector could have made a mistake when he counseled me to remain in the Scalabrinian seminary.

Despite my growing doubts about the rightness of a Scalabrinian vocation for me, I continued to apply myself energetically to the rigors of seminary life. Prayer and study became my most important activities. I was hungry for knowledge, and the classes intrigued me—languages, philosophy, psychology, literature, and theology.

In my life of prayer, I felt I was beginning to walk in the Presence of God. This led me to new and deeper reflections on the nature and purpose of the role I was preparing to fill. Around this time, I committed some of my thoughts to paper; I offer a sample of my early writing now. It reveals the state of my inner thoughts at that time.

❖

PRIESTHOOD

Here I Am.

Here I am in the seminary. What is my aim? What is my ambition?

I want to be a priest. A priest, *sacerdos dans sacra,* one who will give to man the realities of the invisible world: the grace of God. *Sacerdos in aeternum,* a priest not for time but for eternity.

Do I realize fully what this means? To give the grace of God! To give divine life to souls! Who am I to do this! How infused I should be with the supernatural during my years at the seminary. One can give only what one has—particularly in the realm of the supernatural.

To give the Word of God! How earnestly I must prepare, not only to master the art of speaking, but also to understand sound doctrine, that my words may be convincing, inspiring, and compelling!

To give the Pardon of God! I shall have to cleanse souls of sin. How carefully I must first train myself to avoid the least fault; and what is even more, to acquire the highest perfection.

To give the Body of God! How I should cherish everything pertaining to the sacrifice of the altar!

Here I am. I offer you all the sacrifices my vocation may require, particularly the one still so present in my mind—the farewell to my parents.

Ecce venio, I am here, Lord, I am here to accomplish Your Holy Will, to answer Your loving but firm invitation—this mysterious attraction You have deigned to make me feel and which reveals so much love on Your part.

Ecce venio, I would like to put as much spirit into my offering as Mary put into hers the day her vocation was revealed to her; *Ecce Ancilla,* or as You did, O Jesus, the day You offered Yourself on the cross for us to the Most High.

❖

By the end of my first year in the seminary, I had matured closer to God through discipline, meditation, and prayer. I had learned how to pray. This was the period when my life of formal prayer became fuller and richer. I stepped onward, closer to the life of prayer I now experience in the Healing Ministry.

My life of prayer and my interest in my studies sustained me through the four years I spent at Sacred Heart Seminary. I never lost my doubts about the validity of a Scalabrinian vocation for myself, but I was grateful for the pure, ascetic life the Scalabrini Fathers taught me to lead.

In 1949, after four years at Sacred Heart, I was assigned to St. Charles Seminary on Staten Island, New York, to begin my novitiate. Here, again, I was beset with doubts and questions. Though the life was rigorous, I always felt there was great value in that kind of rigor. My problem was still with the particular type of priestly duties I was going to be limited to as a Scalabrini Father.

In my novitiate and philosophy days, there was much turmoil among American students, and it affected me very deeply, for I took such things very seriously. When Scalabrini clerics came from Italy to join the faculty, their ideas and ways clashed with ours. When we observed these differences, some of us realized that there was a profound conflict between their Italian mentality and our American mentality. We tried to make it work, but all the time I saw more and more clearly that it couldn't work for many of us, myself included. But by that time I had gone deeper and deeper into my studies, and I had already taken my religious vows. And when you are in vows, you don't want to disappoint God by going back on your word.

In 1953, after four years of novitiate and philosophy, I left Staten Island and returned to Chicago for four years of theology. I was twenty-three years old, and had completed eight years of arduous training.

Since leaving home at fifteen, I'd grown in spirit, mind and body. My health was generally good, except for an intestinal problem which first appeared in my second year at St. Charles. It interfered with my studies, but after a while it subsided and I thought no more about it.

The year after I returned to Chicago, I had one of the most profound experiences of my life. It began when I first noticed I was bleeding internally. This serious discovery was followed by four hemorrhages in one twenty-four-hour period. Early in the morning I was rushed to the hospital where the doctors diagnosed my illness as intestinal cancer. They gave me four months to live *after* surgery, which had to be performed immediately.

Several of the faculty had accompanied me to the hospital that morning. Of them all, I most clearly remember my vice-rector, Father Scola. I especially esteemed him for his priestly manner and for his scholastic and theological mind.

As they wheeled me into surgery, I was already under sedation. They paused at the door of the operating room. Father Scola came over to me. He had tears in his eyes. He blessed me, then bent over and kissed me. His deep concern for me was inspirational. I held his hand as tightly as I could. I said: "Father, pray that if I'm going to be a bad priest, that God make me die. But if God is calling me to be a special priest for Him, then pray for me to live." Then they wheeled me into the operating room. I have never forgotten that moment.

I was smiling in the operating room because I was so much at peace. I felt no fear. As they were preparing my body for the operation, I noticed through a small window in the operating-room door that my vice-rector and my rector were both there looking in at me. They blessed me. That was the last thing I saw or remembered. The anesthesia took effect immediately. I fell into unconsciousness.

When the surgeons opened my intestines, they found no cancer. All they did was remove a small piece of my intestine that was damaged beyond repair. After the operation, my recuperation seemed to proceed well, but two months later I started to bleed again. The doctors were perplexed: had cancer really taken root, as previously diagnosed? But time passed, and with medical care and God's help, my intestinal problem subsided.

This experience was doubly profound. In the first instance, I'd asked Father Scola to pray for my recovery only if God was calling me to be a special priest for Him. I took my recovery as an indication that God planned some special use for me in the future.

The second profound lesson lay in the fact that I had experienced the threat of fatal illness and imminent death from the point of view of the victim. I was sensitized to the suffering of the sick. This sensitivity prepared me for my eventual use in the Healing Ministry.

It was only years later that the cause of my intestinal disorder was diagnosed. As it turned out, I'd contracted a serious amoebic infection, probably from one of the seminarians, an older man who had a late vocation. He'd picked up the infection in South America and for reasons of hygiene was assigned a private toilet. But one of my duties at the seminary was to clean the toilets, his included, and that was probably how I contracted the infection. At the time, I did not see the connection myself. And since it was a rare kind of infection to be found in Chicago, the doctors did not look for it and so did not find it. Nevertheless, the infection was inside me, slowly eating away at my intestines.

Eventually I recovered from that first intestinal attack and the surgery I underwent. I resumed my studies and training, once more back on the path toward becoming a priest. In the final year or two of my training, time seemed to pass more quickly. By now I was totally engrossed in the life of prayer and study. Each day brought me closer to God and my goal of becoming a priest. And so the time passed until finally the Big Day arrived, the day toward which I'd been striving for twelve years, the day on which I would be ordained a Roman Catholic priest.

Three

THOU ART
A PRIEST FOREVER

Saturday, June 1, 1957, was the day of days. Though I went to bed Friday night, I did not sleep. I lay in the dark waiting for the night to pass. But the anticipation and excitement which filled my heart seemed to make time stand still. When I realized I would get no sleep that night, I got out of bed at 4 A.M.

After washing and dressing, I composed myself and calmly walked to the clerics' chapel. It was to be the last time I would kneel in that beautiful small chapel where, for so many years, heart spoke to heart. And there, in that familiar place, on the morning of my ordination, I spent my holy hour alone with my King.

My heart was grateful, and a sense of humility at my nothingness permeated my whole being. He was about to ordain me His forever. Can anyone but a fellow priest imagine the meaning of that, or experience the depth of my feeling? *"A priest forever . . . forever . . . forever."*

A priest. To become a priest. But what is a priest? And, more specifically, what is a priest to Christians?

To be a priest means to be Christ, to perpetuate Christ just as He is throughout time and space. The priest is not merely someone or something. He is *The One*. The priest *Is Christ*, and consequently he is the most necessary one. If it is true that one thing only is necessary in life, the salvation of one's soul, then the priest is the most necessary one, because salvation is only through the priest.

Christ, after His resurrection, did not confine His priesthood to a celestial intercession on our behalf. He has willed to exercise His priesthood here in the world through the priests.

By virtue of the divine power conferred upon Him by the sacrament of the Holy Orders, the priest becomes a living personification of Christ. He no longer acts in his own name. It is Christ who acts in him, who lives and works in him. When a priest baptizes, he does not say, "May God baptize you," but, "I baptize you." He does not say, "May God forgive you your sins," but, "I forgive you." Nor does he say, "This is blood and body of Christ," but, "This is my body. This is my blood."

The priest, man of God, remains a man. He has no family, yet he belongs to every family. No one comes into this world or goes hence without him. He takes a child from the arms of its mother, and he parts with him or her only at the grave. He blesses and consecrates the cradle, the bridal room, the bed of death, and the bier.

The priest is one whom innocent children grow to love. Even those who do not know him salute him as "Father." He is the one at whose feet Christians kneel and lay the innermost thoughts of their souls—the secrets of their hearts of which no one dares to inquire. It is to him they weep their most sacred tears.

Until the end of time, the priest will be the most beloved and the most hated of men, the dearest brother and the arch enemy. He is one whose name is love. He was invented by Love for love. He has abandoned everything. He has given all. But there is one thing which he does retain which will never be given away, which nothing can make him relinquish. And this is *Love*, because His name is Love.

This is the Catholic priesthood.

I was overwhelmed by the realization that I myself would be ordained a priest in a few hours. In a flash of insight, I saw and understood that all the sacrifices of the past twelve years and all the sacrifices I would be called on to make in the future were worth it and would always be worth it. As testimony to that insight, in a few hours I would be ordained. From the sacrifices of the past, a Sacrament was to be made.

With a heart full of gratitude, I thanked my God. Tears of joy and thankfulness welled up in me. As my last act of devotion in the familiar chapel where I had so frequently prayed, I consecrated anew all of myself to be His—my physical body, my mind, my soul, and my spirit, which I asked Him to fill with more hope, faith, and love.

The ordination ceremony was scheduled for nine o'clock in the morning in Mother Cabrini Church on Sacramento Boulevard in Chicago. The pews were crowded with relatives, friends, and well-wishers. Everyone seemed to share in the sacred meaning of the rite that was about to begin.

My classmates and I knelt in the humility of our nothingness before the large stone altar of St. Francis. There were five of us—Vince, Ed, Chuck, Mike, and myself. Each of us was lost in his private awareness of this most fulfilling moment of our lives.

The world seemed different to me, as if everything were taking special note of the occasion. Even the air I inhaled was unforgettable. The altar was bedecked with fresh flowers which filled the church with their aroma. The holy oils, with which our hands would soon be anointed, gave off their special fragrance. The sweet-smelling holy wine and the fresh scent of bread made from wheat rose up and blended with the other aromas to create a kind of perfumed background for the mysterious event about to unfold—the ordination of new Catholic priests.

Bishop Raymond J. Hillinger, D.D., God rest his soul, approached the sanctuary. He and his attendants were magnificent in their ceremonial raiment. With great dignity, the Bishop, a large, imposing figure of a man, began the ordination ceremony. His manly voice—deep, profound, articulate —echoed forth throughout the church in the succinct, beautiful language of Latin: *"Tu es sacerdos aeternum.* You are a priest forever."

Again those words struck a deep response in my soul. "A

priest forever." It was a precious gift. And it hadn't come easily. The cost of priesthood is high. The price is our surrender.

The sacrament of Holy Orders would make me a priest, but then the priest would become the sacrament. The Bishop's words of admonition rang clearly in my ears and continue to echo even more strongly now: "Dearly beloved sons, you are about to be ordained to the order of the priesthood. Strive to receive it worthily and, after having received it, to perform its duties in a praiseworthy manner. The office of the priest is to offer sacrifice, to bless, to govern, to preach, to baptize, and to heal the sick."

The Bishop's words impressed themselves upon me with great clarity and strength. They were words with which I would live forever. My attention was focused on him as he continued the prayer of the Church.

"Hear us, we pray, O Lord God, and pour out on these servants of Yours the blessing of the Holy Spirit and the power of priestly grace. And now as we present them for consecration in Your benign presence, may You sustain them forever by the bounty of Your gifts . . . we pray that You bestow on these servants of Yours the dignity of the priesthood. Renew in their hearts the spirit of holiness . . . may they be prudent fellow workers in our ministry. May they shine in all virtues, so that they will be able to give a good account of the stewardship entrusted to them . . . may it please You, O Lord, to consecrate and sanctify these hands by this anointing and our blessing . . . that whatever they bless may be blessed, and whatever they consecrate may be consecrated in the name of Our Lord Jesus Christ."

Earlier that morning I had hoped my chalice would be used by the ordaining Bishop during the ceremony. It is a unique chalice, having been designed by my father and me and dedicated to Our Lady of Lourdes. When the moment came, the Bishop did select my chalice and used it in the ceremony.

While awaiting my turn for the consecration of my hands,

I whispered to the Lord, "God, I hope the Bishop uses a lot of oil on my hands." But when I approached and knelt before him, Bishop Hillinger routinely dipped his finger into the consecrating oil and withdrew it with a meager amount. He started to consecrate my hands. "O Lord," I thought, "how sparing he is with the oil."

Suddenly the Bishop said to his attendants, "Oh, I think I made a verbal mistake by not reading the proper words." Thereupon he hurriedly dipped his large thumb into the vessel of consecrated oil, spilling some of it about himself, then took my hands and soaked them with the sacred oil. With a smile I said to the Lord, *"Deo gratias."*

And so the good Bishop anointed our hands with the holy oil: "May it please You, O Lord, to consecrate and sanctify these hands by this anointing and our blessing." After making the sign of the cross over our hands, he added, "May whatever they bless be blessed, and may whatever they consecrate be consecrated in the name of Our Lord Jesus Christ." The assistants wrapped our anointed hands with white cloth.

The Bishop then presented each of us with a chalice containing the wine and water. On top of the chalice was a paten containing a host. As we touched the paten and the cup of the chalice with our fore and middle fingers, the Bishop proclaimed, "Receive the power to offer sacrifice to God and to celebrate masses for the living and the dead." The great power to offer the Eucharist, to offer love to love, had been imparted to us.

The Bishop sat on the folding stool at the middle of the altar. As I approached him, I took note of the exact time— 9:17 A.M. I knelt alone before this holy Bishop. He lifted his huge hands and placed them firmly on my head. His voice was deep, heavy with meaning: "Receive the Holy Spirit. Whose sins you shall forgive, they are forgiven them; whose sins you shall retain, they are retained." Finally the consolation for man's weaknesses, the power to absolve sins, became ours.

At that moment the priestly garment called the chasuble, which up to then I had worn folded on my shoulders, was unfolded and dropped over my back, while the Bishop proclaimed, "The Lord clothe you with the robe of innocence."

As the Bishop spoke these words, the angelic voices of the choir swelled majestically through the church: "*Ecce sacerdos novus!* Behold a new priest!"

While the singing filled the air, words spoken by Pius XII to the Catholic priesthood came to my mind: "You priests are 'Our Glory and Joy.' You, who with such great generosity, bear the 'burden of the day and the heat.' If, however, your work is to be blessed by God and produce abundant fruit, it must be rooted in holiness of life. Sanctity is the chief and most important endowment of the Catholic priest. Without it, other charisms will not go far. With it, even supposing other gifts be meager, the priest can work marvels."

As soon as the Bishop concluded the service, hundreds of people rushed the newly ordained priests—friends, relatives, benefactors, congregants. They came asking for our first priestly blessings. As I was being thronged by a host of people asking for my first priestly blessing, all I remember saying was, "Yes, I will bless you. I will bless all of you. But please, please, my first blessing to my mother." And so I went to my mother and to my father to impart my first blessing upon them. My mother, dressed in a white suit, knelt before me. I blessed her first and Dad second. Some of the observers stood in awe. Others cried. But we weren't sad. We were full of happiness and gratitude.

And so it was. I was now a priest forever.

Four

CHICAGO
APOSTOLATE

When I returned to Providence in June 1957, I went home as a priest. My friends and the rest of my family got to see me as an ordained priest for the first time. It was there in Providence, before a church full of familiar faces on Father's Day, June 15, that I celebrated my first mass.

I was then a month short of my twenty-seventh birthday. Many of the boys and girls I'd grown up with were now married and already raising families of their own. When I used to come home on vacation, some of these old childhood friends and acquaintances would suggest I leave the seminary. "You've been at it ten years, Ralph; where's it going to get you?"

They advised me to try my luck in the secular world. They asked about seminary life and suggested I leave it because they couldn't see where my life was headed. But when they came to church and witnessed me saying the mass in my new role as a Roman Catholic priest, they finally saw and understood where I'd been heading all those long years. Then they congratulated me with warmth and love.

My stay in Providence that June was refreshing; I had a month of vacation between ordination and first assignment. I renewed several old friendships and spent much of my time with my parents, my brother, and my sister. But I was eager for my vacation to end so I could finally begin my full-time duties as a Scalabrini missionary priest.

For reasons of organization, the Scalabrini congregation has divided the world into provinces, each of which is presided over by an administrator known as a Provincial. Every six years the provincials gather in Rome and elect one of their number to serve as Superior General. The Superior General acts as the worldwide chief executive of the Scalabrini congregation and holds office for six years, until the next election.

The Superior General makes the decisions about issues which lie outside the boundaries of any particular province, but within each province, the local provincial has a good deal of autonomy. The Superior General, for example, has the responsibility for making all assignments to specific provinces, but once a Scalabrinian has been assigned, he's mostly under the authority of his Provincial, who makes all assignments within a province.

My first formal letter of assignment arrived at my parents' house one June morning. I quickly opened it and learned that I'd been assigned to the Western province of the United States. (The United States is divided into two Scalabrinian provinces, the Eastern and the Western. My assignment to the Western province was in accord with the prevailing tradition in religious orders and congregations to assign priests to serve in places other than their home regions.) Within the Western province, I was assigned to St. Michael's parish in Chicago as a summer replacement.

Many blessings were bestowed upon me during my months in St. Michael's. The two most enduring and meaningful of my experiences came about through two men—my pastor, Father Louis Dananzan, and a Communist immigrant from Tuscany named Mario.

Father Louis remains one of the most dedicated, socially conscious men I've ever known. He was already a man of great experience when I was fortunate enough to have him as my pastor, and he shared his experience with me as a respected teacher shares with a respectful student. Father Louis showed me *how* to help people who needed help. He taught me that bringing God to people often had to start with bringing food, medicine, and jobs, if those things were needed. That was the beginning of bringing God to people.

Father Louis was a man of many interests and diverse duties. Among other things, he was involved in a religious radio program. The things I learned from him about the possibilities of radio came to fruition a few years later when I did a religious radio program in Utica, New York. More recently, his influence surfaced again in the radio and television facets of our current Healing Ministry.

Whenever he was called away on duties outside the parish, which happened with some frequency, he unhesitatingly left me in charge. I was barely three months out of the seminary, and when he left the parish in my hands, I could feel my confidence growing. Perhaps Father Louis' demonstration of faith in my abilities was the greatest blessing he bestowed upon me.

St. Michael's parish is on the West Side of Chicago. In those days, its ethnic composition was made up mostly of Tuscans, or *Toscani*, as they are called in Italian. These people were from Tuscany, a province of northern Italy famous for the beauty of its land and the culture and refinement of its people. Florence, the major city of Tuscany, is known as the home of the purest form of the Italian language—*la lingua madre*.

The Toscani living in St. Michael's parish spoke the Italian language with a precise beauty that I had rarely heard before, and I looked forward to improving my own conversational Italian as I worked with them. These people also possessed rich backgrounds in art, literature, and, above all, opera. Their knowledge and appreciation of culture was very wide.

But there was also great poverty among the Toscani, most of whom had come to the States after World War II. In many cases, they hadn't been in America long enough to find decent, well-paying work. When they found work, it was usually at low wages or as self-employed small businessmen, trying to eke out a bare living.

In many cases, their living conditions were barely adequate. Some only had meager food; some were sickly. Later, when I assumed my role as an active participant in the social fabric of this community, one of the things I did was to contact employers and explain the situation. I managed to get jobs for some of the new arrivals.

Eventually I got to know the Toscani quite well, but in the beginning, I knew very little about them. Among the things I didn't know was the fact that many of them were Communists who had rejected the Church as irrelevant and who hated priests, whom they viewed as their enemies in the class struggle. Though I was unaware of these sentiments in the very beginning, I learned of them quickly enough.

The way I found out and the manner in which I conducted myself is typical of the way I usually respond to new people or situations; I'm open and always willing to think the best of someone until he shows me otherwise. What have I to lose? By assuming the best, I open myself to a new experience and retain the right to change my mind. If I assume the worst before actually knowing a person, I close myself off from an experience without ever giving it a chance, and who knows what blessing might have come from such a lost opportunity?

One of the first things I did in St. Michael's parish was to walk through the streets. I wanted to meet the people and let them see me. I made it a habit on those walks to step into stores and introduce myself.

On one of my first walks I passed a barber shop. Through the window I noticed a group of eight or ten men in animated conversation. I stepped in. As soon as they saw me, their conversation stopped. Not only that, their mouths virtually dropped open, as if they'd just had a great surprise.

The men seemed to eye my clothes very suspiciously, but I wasn't wearing anything unusual, only the ordinary Roman collar and black suit of a Catholic priest.

I was slightly perplexed by their reaction, but I smiled and said hello in Italian. I thought it would be a good opportunity to practice conversational Italian with some men who spoke it in its purest form. With the clearest pronunciation

I was capable of, I said in Italian, "I'd like to get a haircut, if I may."

For some reason I couldn't grasp, something about me seemed to make them uneasy. But finally I drew them into conversation. We talked about jobs and the kinds of problems they encountered when they tried to find work. I could discuss work issues in a way that revealed I knew something about the subject. My own working-class background helped me understand their experiences and point of view.

The men were cautious, but before long we had a lively conversation in progress while I had my haircut. As I left, one of the men walked out the door with me. "You're a different kind of priest," he said; "you're down to earth."

When I got home, Father Louis said, "I see you had a haircut." He asked me where I'd gotten it. When I described the barber shop, a smile of amazement lit his face, and he exclaimed, "There! You went there? Do you know where you've been? That's the hangout of the strongest Communist group in the vicinity!"

As soon as Father Louis mentioned their politics, I understood at once why the men had behaved so strangely; they couldn't believe a priest would walk right into their lair, so to speak.

When I thought about the scene in light of my new knowledge, the humor of it spilled forth in a long laugh, which I shared with Father Louis. "You know," I said, when our laughter had subsided, "the barber didn't even want to take my money for the haircut." And we laughed again.

✽

As part of my duties, I frequently visited Toscani families. Sometimes I ate meals with them, blessed their homes, discussed their children. In this way I got to know them better, and they me.

Often I'd stroll up and down the streets of the neighborhood, saying hello and striking up brief conversations. In this unobtrusive way, I was able to take an informal census of the neighborhood, meeting the people and identifying their needs so they could be ministered to adequately.

One day I stepped into a small cleaning and pressing shop I'd never noticed before. Though unaware of it at the time, this was the start of my extraordinary encounter with an immigrant named Mario. The shop was one of those marginal businesses from which the owner and his family try desperately to eke out a living.

A woman and a small boy, clearly her son, were standing there. They were both blue-eyed and fair-skinned, genuine Toscani. I introduced myself, and we struck up a conversation. As we talked, I learned that the woman was deeply religious and wished to raise her son to follow her example. But her husband, a young man named Mario, was a Communist. He hated the Church, and he was dying of cancer.

I commiserated with the poor woman, then asked if I could see her husband. She led me to the rear of the shop, pushed aside a curtain which had been hung to divide the space into two rooms, and we stepped into Mario's bedroom.

It was a small, dingy space. He was lying in bed. His wife introduced me, and he looked up at me with suspicion in his eyes. His face was gaunt with the ravages of disease.

I pulled up a chair and sat down beside him. I made no mention of God, church, or religion. After a few moments, his wife returned to the front of the store to attend to a customer. Alone with Mario, I continued my informal conversation. I complimented him on his wife and child and told him some of the neighborhood news. He relaxed his guard a little and asked a few questions about this one or that one.

Before I left, I asked, "Mario, can I visit you again, as a friend?"

He looked up at me and said, *"Si, Padre.* Yes, Father, please do."

So I took to dropping by. Sometimes I'd bring some fruit or a candy bar for the little boy. I'd pull up the same chair every time, and we'd talk about people in the neighborhood or the way in which America differed from Italy. Mario even told me some stories about his childhood.

For three or four months our conversation took place at least once a week. We talked about many things, but Mario never mentioned his politics, and I never mentioned my religion. Our relationship continued on this carefully limited basis until the first Friday in October, when some force inside me led me to break the pattern.

On the first Friday of each month I made communion calls to the sick and housebound. Normally on days I was giving communion I didn't stop at Mario's. But this day, as I drove from one house to another, I felt a pressure in my mind, as if I'd forgotten an errand. But I couldn't recall anything I was supposed to do.

Then a kind of awesome spirit came over me, making me feel suddenly grave and serious, and a voice inside me said, "Go to Mario. Go to Mario." As soon as I finished my scheduled communion calls, I drove to the store and quickly got out of the car.

I felt as if a force was propelling me forward. I entered the store, parted the curtain, and walked directly into Mario's bedroom. He looked more haggard than ever, but there was surprise on his face; I'd never burst in on him like this.

Before he could utter his surprise, I began to speak. The words seemed to come out of my mouth of their own accord. "Mario! Do you want to return to God?"

I spoke so loudly, it was almost a shout. His eyes became very intense. He did not take them from my face as I continued to speak.

"Mario," I said, "I've never talked to you about God, the Church, or the sacrament. But something inside of me told me to come to you today, on this special day dedicated to the Sacred Heart of Jesus. And tomorrow, the first Saturday of the month, is dedicated to the Immaculate Heart of Mary. It is an auspicious time, Mario. God seems to be telling me that he wants you to make your confession. I ask you, Mario, will you make your peace with God?"

He looked at me for only a moment, then said in a very

quiet voice, "*Si, Padre, si. Immediatemente.* Yes, Father. Immediately!"

As soon as he said yes, I took out my stole, slipped it over my shoulders, and heard his confession. But I could not offer him Holy Communion because I had no communion wafers left. I'd given them out on my earlier stops. Mario accepted my offer to return the next day and give him Holy Communion.

The next day, as I'd told Mario, would be dedicated to the Immaculate Heart of Mary. As if by Divine Coincidence, the Immaculate Heart of Mary had requested the world to pray for the conversion of Russia back to the Heart of Christ, especially for the conversion of atheistic Communists.

I saw Mario at the eleventh hour of his life, a life he'd dedicated to atheistic Communism, suddenly desiring to return to the hands of his Maker. Truly, God is a God of mercy and love.

The next morning, after completing my other communion calls, I drove to Mario's. Before getting out of the car, I made certain I had a communion wafer for Mario.

All morning I had rushed so I could get to Mario. By ten-thirty I was at his side. I took the Host from its special container and held it in my right hand. We Catholics believe the Host is Jesus Christ, made so through the mystery of transubstantiation. Mario stared at the Host, transfixed, as I began to recite:

"Behold the Lamb of God. Behold Him Who comes in the name of the Lord. This is the Body of Christ . . . *Dominus noster Jesus Christus custodiat* . . . May our Lord Jesus Christ guide you on to eternal life. Amen."

With the Host held in my hand, I made the sign of the Cross. As I reached out to place the Host in Mario's mouth, he suddenly lunged up from his pillow and clutched my right wrist with both his hands.

His hands were bony from the ravages of cancer, but they had a strength I would not have believed possible. His fingernails dug into my flesh with all the strength left in his dying body; he gasped, "Jesus, forgive me all my sins. I beg of you one thing. Let me die. My wife and my son are tortured by my slow agony. Let me die at once, Jesus, to end their suffering."

Mario struggled for breath and whispered hoarsely, *"Perdonami! Perdonami! Dio mio, perdonami!* Have mercy on me! Have mercy on me! My God, My God!"

As he whispered these words, his fingers released their fierce grip on my wrist, and his head dropped back to his pillow. He was exhausted. But there was a new light in his eyes, a clearer gaze. I gave him Holy Communion and left.

At the parish house a few hours later I received a call from his wife. She was crying. "Father," she said, "Mario just died."

Three days later I celebrated the funeral mass for Mario. I preached the story of his life, a life which returned to God at the eleventh hour of its earthly existence and found God waiting with outstretched arm and opened hand. Another prodigal son had returned.

Mario's life demonstrated once again the infinite mercy of God's love for each and every one of his children. And God's great message illuminated the darkness of Mario's death: When the eternal peace of an immortal soul is at stake, it's never too late to return to God.

Five

NEIGHBORHOODS
OF CHICAGO

Shortly after the death of Mario, my temporary assignment at St. Michael's parish came to an end. I felt some regrets; I still had more to learn from Father Louis Dananzan, and I was just beginning to establish meaningful contacts among the Toscani in the parish.

Although I felt some regret, a part of me liked the idea of change. I looked forward to the challenge of entering a new situation and meeting new people. At that time of my life I wanted to travel and experience new places, because I believed such experiences would enlarge my concepts of the priesthood and broaden my priestly abilities.

As it turned out, my missionary priesthood with the Scalabrini Fathers provided ample opportunity for new experiences. The brief duration of my very first assignment set a pattern that was to continue throughout all the years I was a Scalabrini Father. At first I found the frequent reassignments exciting, but as time passed I began to feel the need for more permanence. I wanted to establish roots in a community and become part of its total fabric so I could bring my vision of a holistic ministry to the people I was serving.

In the long run, the lack of a permanent assignment was one of the causative factors which led to my withdrawal from the Scalabrini congregation, my becoming a diocesan priest, and eventually led me to the Healing Ministry, the focal point of my life. But at the beginning of my priesthood, I liked the challenge of new situations and experiences. So it was with keen expectation that I looked forward to my new assignment, which carried me to the South Side of Chicago into the Santa Maria Addolorata parish in the role of second assistant pastor.

My assignment to Sta. Maria was labeled "permanent," but an emergency arose which shortened it to four months. Nevertheless, during my stay at Sta. Maria, my expectations were fulfilled with new experiences, people, and knowledge.

The day I arrived, I walked in the front door of the rectory with my valise in one hand and my chalice in the other. The housekeeper announced me, and Father Alex Peloso, the pastor, and Father Joseph Favotto, the first assistant pastor, came bounding down the stairs.

Father Alex, an extraordinarily energetic man, clasped my shoulder and almost shouted, *"Bienvenido, Raffaello!* Welcome to Santa Maria." Father Joseph, whom I had known twelve years earlier as my Italian language teacher at the seminary, joined in the warm welcome.

They made me feel at home immediately, but before I could catch my breath and respond, Father Alex quickly said to Father Joe, "Take his luggage, then take him right down to the sports store and get him a ball—he's going out with the team tonight. In fact, Father Ralph doesn't know it yet, but he's going to take care of the whole bowling league!" Father Alex looked at me with a big smile, and the next thing I knew, I was in a car with Father Joe on my way to get fitted for my own personal bowling ball. And I thought to myself, "I've done many things for the Lord, all done freely with love and to the best of my ability, but this is a new one on me. But if I have to bowl for the Lord, then bowl I will, and I hope I bowl a lot of strikes."

The Young Men's Bowling Club, for which I was responsible, was typical of Father Alex's pastoral style; he was a man committed to the belief that the practical aspects of life are not to be spurned, for these practical aspects are frequently stepping-stones to things of higher value. He also understood the value of the practical approach. He seemed to be a man who could get anything for the people.

Father Alex's reputation as a man who got things done was well known. In one five-year period, he had relocated a church into a new physical complex consisting of a new church, rectory, and school. And it was all paid for. He was an administrator and an organizer well worth holding up as a model, and in this role he exerted a great influence on my future development.

He also served as a living corrective. During my seminary years of deep study and prayer, I'd grown somewhat distanced from the practical realities of life. The mundane but absolutely necessary material needs of existence had slipped slightly from the focus of my attention. As a result of my intense spiritual and theological concerns, I'd begun to overlook the material needs of people. Father Alex put an end to this error immediately and pointed me back in the direction of my own life experiences. He put me back in touch with my childhood and the practical realities of growing up in a family where the material necessities had not always come easily.

Father Alex, as was natural, covered the administrative duties. Father Joe was in charge of the traditional pastoral needs of the parish—the Holy Name Society, home and hospital visits to the sick or housebound, that type of routine. And I, being the youngest, was assigned to youth work.

In the life of a young priest, youth work provides a unique opportunity for giving genuine service to others while at the same time experiencing invaluable, necessary personal growth. The greatest advantage a young priest has in working with young people is his own youthfulness; though his training and education have set him somewhat apart from the youth he is serving, a young priest is still close enough in age to his young flock to understand their concerns, problems, and interests. Not all young priests, however, are given the opportunity to work with youth, and I'll always remain thankful to Father Alex for giving me that chance.

Father Alex believed youth work to be one of the most important of our priestly duties, for youth not only represent the future, they *are* the future. When he gave me the assignment, he expected results.

I also took the assignment seriously. My first step was to evaluate the youth needs and the youth services available in our South Side parish. As has always been my style, I went out among the people to learn about conditions.

Out on the streets, one of the first sights which met my eyes were groups of kids hanging around on corners or in front of such places as poolrooms or saloons. They behaved like would-be gangsters or, at the very least, like potential juvenile delinquents. As soon as I learned that many of the men who frequented these places were actual gangsters and petty hoodlums, I knew something constructive had to be done for the kids, or else they might be drawn into lives of crime and dissipation.

Acting quickly, and with Father Alex's approval, I invited a few of the street-corner kids to help me clean out an unused room in the basement of the church, which they could then use. I knew that my immediate goal was to draw them to God. But as yet I had no clear idea how to implement this goal. I improvised, one step at a time.

Before long the basement room was cleared, painted, refurnished, and decorated as a clubhouse. Activities developed at the request of the boys themselves. A hobby shop was set up in the back, music groups sprang up, and we even began a choir.

The variety of activities allowed us to use any interest or talent a youth might have in order to draw him in and point him toward God. One afternoon I met a particularly ragged boy on the street. He acted tough and was very cautious in his conversation with me, but I thought I detected a note of interest in his voice. So I tried to draw him in:

"Would you like to help me serve mass?"

"No," he mumbled.

"Interested in baking or cooking?"

"Uh-uh."

"Want to make something in our shop?"

He shook his head. I thought for a moment. "Well, can you sing?"

He smiled. "Yes, Father, I can sing."

"Good," I answered, "You're in my choir."

"All right, Father. I'll be there," he said. And he was. His talent for singing brought him a step closer to God.

The boys' club thrived. At Christmas we held a ceremony to invest all the boys as Knights of the Altar, with cassock and surplice. I even dubbed them with a sword. It was a gratifying evening. The boys were exhilarated, and their parents, most of whom attended the ceremony, were thankful that their sons had been taken off the streets.

When the club started, I had eight or ten boys between the ages of nine and thirteen. Before I left, I had over sixty boys, many of whom followed me everywhere I went. They visited me at the rectory, always eager to do errands or lend a hand, and they liked to accompany me on sick calls. If they saw me heading for my car, one would shout, "Hey, Father Ralph! Where are you going?"

"On a sick call. A man is dying."

"Can we come?"

"Come on, but be quick about it. Jump in the car."

After my call, we'd visit an ice-cream parlor or take a walk in the neighborhood.

Whatever we happened to be doing, many of these boys liked to be around me. I was always straightforward with them and treated them fairly. I tried to emulate the behavior of the adults in my own life whom I'd found most nourishing—relatives, teachers, or clergy. In response to my openness and enthusiasm, the boys grew attached to me. But I never lost sight of the fact that in a deeper and truer sense, they were forming an attachment to God, whose priest and conduit I am. The priest is the visible manifestation of the invisible Glory of God, and as such it is his role to draw people and point them toward that which the limitations of our human condition prevents us from seeing.

There was a boy whose story clearly demonstrated the way in which a priest serves as intercessor between man and God. I'll call the boy Billy; he came from a broken home and he was full of hurt and anger. Not knowing any other way, he channeled his pain and rage into antisocial actions, and he was well on his way to becoming a full-fledged juvenile delinquent when I met him.

Billy was a student in the parochial school of the parish. When I learned he was continually getting into trouble, I decided to make an effort to save him. I always picked the most troubled boys because they obviously were the ones who needed the most help.

I went to the Sister in charge of Billy's class and told her I wanted to train Billy to be one of my altar boys. The Sister was a very competent woman, and I respected her years of experience and knowledge, but she seemed to think I was a naive young man with visions of grandeur about my abilities. "My dear Father," she said, looking slightly down her nose, "you are a young priest, and I've had many years of experience. I tell you, this child is headed for a fall."

I was taken by surprise. All I did by way of answering was to shrug my shoulders.

"Billy would not make a good altar boy," the Sister continued. "He's got too many problems."

I didn't doubt his problems for one moment, but I did doubt the flat prediction of his failure. Wasn't Billy's opportunity for personal achievement, just like his opportunity for eternal salvation, always just around the corner? Wasn't it *possible* that Billy would let me help him redirect his pain and anguish away from antisocial behavior and toward our compassionate Lord, Who suffers all our pains?

I wanted to try, but I needed Sister's cooperation. "May I have him?" I asked.

"If you insist, Father."

"It's not a matter of insisting. All I want to do is train him to be an altar boy."

"Well, when he slips up here in school, I'll be sure to

let you know about it. Will you do the same?"

"Certainly, Sister, but may he join my altar boys?"

"Yes, Father, Billy may join, but don't say I didn't warn you."

I spent a great deal of time with Billy, and he made rapid progress. He became an altar boy, one of the best I had. He seemed to be doing very well. Then one day I got a phone call from the school. It was Billy's teacher.

"Father DiOrio?"

"Yes?"

"Do you remember what I told you about Billy before you took him in your program?"

"Yes."

"Well, *your* altar boy is in trouble again. Will you come and handle him? We can't! He'll be out in the corridor."

I put the phone down, got in my car, and drove right over. When I walked into the school, I saw Billy immediately. He was standing before a row of lockers. As the front door closed, Billy looked up the corridor and saw me walking toward him. He did not know that Sister had phoned me and that I already knew about his trouble. All he knew was that he didn't want me to see him. So he jumped into a locker and closed the door.

I walked up to the locker and softly knocked on the door. No answer.

I knocked again. "Hello, Billy! I know you're in there. You might as well come out."

He opened the door. His face was red, and tears streamed from his eyes.

"Why are you crying, Billy?" I asked. "Why did you hide in the locker?"

"Because I'm ashamed. You've been good to me, Father Ralph, and now I've gotten in trouble in school and I've let you down. And I know when I let you down, I let God down too. Forgive me, Father Ralph, and I'll pray that God forgives me too."

I looked at the boy, but I was too moved to speak. I put

my arm around his shoulder, gave him a hug, and we walked down the corridor together.

❖

Our youth programs flourished. Among other groups we had the Boys' Club, the Knights of the Altar, the Girls' Choir, the Teen Club, and the Bowling Club. Some of the counseling I provided was handled in a more or less formal way, but I believe most of my counseling was delivered during informal contact in the club room or at a bowling alley.

Bowling and other social activities were full of brief serious moments, moments during which genuine pastoral duties were performed. A youngster might approach me at the water cooler, for example, and ask quietly, "Father, can I talk with you a minute? I've got something on my mind."

In instances such as these, a word of advice or encouragement might be enough. If not, an appointment was made for a later time. Either way, it was an easy, low-pressure setting in which to approach a priest for help. This style of easy accessibility was modeled to a great extent on the style of Father Piccolo, my boyhood priest back in Providence.

The rectory at Sta. Maria was also readily accessible, and people, young and old, came and went all day long. One particular afternoon, a woman with a child in her arms came to the rectory and began to tell a tale of great need. She looked familiar, but I couldn't place her. She told a jumbled story about acute stomach problems and claimed she was having surgery the next day. Her problem this day was her lack of money to buy food for herself and her child.

At that moment, I suddenly remembered when I'd seen her before. Six months earlier, across town, she had come to the rectory door at St. Michael's with the same child in her arms and the same sad tale of woe on her lips. On that first occasion, I had taken pity and given her the few dollars I had in my pocket. The parish housekeeper also heard the story, and she gave the poor woman six or eight dollars from her pocket. The woman had thanked us and left. Now she was back with the same story.

I didn't let on that I'd recognized her. She obviously didn't recognize me. When she finished her sad tale, the smile I'd been holding back suddenly lit up my face, and I asked, "What happened to the money I gave you six months ago when you told me the same story at St. Michael's?"

She looked me right in the eye and with a perfectly straight face said, "Oh, no, Father, that wasn't me. That was my sister. We're in the same business."

What could I do? I laughed.

✻

After four months—happy and productive months, to be sure—my assignment to the Sta. Maria parish came to an unexpected and sudden end. A fellow priest in another Chicago parish had been stricken with cancer, and it was necessary to transfer him to Sta. Maria, where he could receive the care he required. Soon after, Father Louis Garberine moved in. His condition had not been exaggerated. He was deathly ill and died a year or so later while still in his early thirties. When he moved into Sta. Maria, I moved out and took his place in Holy Guardian Angel parish.

Holy Guardian Angel is on the East Side of Chicago. I believe it's fair to call it one of the most unique parishes in the country, if not in the world. Most of the people in the parish, like most people everywhere, are decent, law-abiding, God-loving folks, but the parish is also the home of a notorious tradition.

Holy Guardian Angel had been the home parish of no less a notorious figure than Scarface Al Capone, the original chief of the mob. I soon learned that some of my parishioners took a strange pride in the infamous characters who had come out of their neighborhood. As a result, I heard many tales of the old days when there had been gun battles on the streets between rival gangs.

The Guardian Angel neighborhood itself was composed

of three-story brick tenements crowded together on narrow streets. Nearby was Polk Street, the street on which Mrs. Murphy's famous cow kicked over the lantern which started the Chicago fire. Other streets were lined with the goods of street peddlers, and some streets were known for their tough boys. A few blocks away was the world-famous settlement house founded by Jane Addams—Hull House. I spent a good deal of time at Hull House; it was a center that enriched the whole area.

The Guardian Angel neighborhood was so interesting that a major Hollywood motion picture was filmed there— *Knock on Any Door*, with Humphrey Bogart and John Derek. The film was made long before I arrived, but I've seen it. The central character of the story is Nick Romana, and the film traces his rise as a gangster. In his boyhood, he is depicted as an altar boy in church, and it was our Holy Guardian Angel Church that they actually used, though they called it "St. Augustine's" in the film.

As I said, it was only a film, but the real-life man on whom the story was based had actually lived in the parish. Some of the Sisters I knew still remembered him. They claimed he had been a very handsome fellow. In the film, Nick Romana had a motto which he quoted frequently, "Live fast, die young, and have a good-looking corpse." He followed his motto in every detail. But in the real life of Holy Guardian Angel parish, this was not exactly an unheard-of event. Some of the older Sisters could recall the Prohibition era, and they told stories about the days of the gang wars when it was not that unusual to wake up in the morning and find a machine-gunned body out front.

As for myself, when I heard the stories about the many gang victims who had been found in the vicinity of the church, I smiled inwardly and wondered how many of them had taken a turn toward God in the final moments of their lives.

Turning people toward God has always been my priority. It was my goal on the day I was ordained, and it is the ultimate goal of the Healing Ministry today. Being healed unto the Lord is the healing that truly counts.

In pursuit of my goal, I've never hesitated to go to the people in need, wherever they may have been. But I had to learn, from practical experience, that church was not the only proper place to carry on God's work. In fact, I learned that God's house exists anywhere His work is being done, and I mean anywhere.

One cold and windy winter afternoon, as I made my way along Michigan Avenue in downtown Chicago with several errands in mind, a police cruiser pulled over, and one of the officers called, "Hi, Father Ralph, how are you doing?"

I recognized him immediately; he was in the Holy Name Society. But I hadn't seen him for a while. I walked over to the cruiser. "Hello, Fred, how are you? I didn't see you at mass Sunday. You're a member of the Holy Name Society, and you missed communion—is anything wrong?"

Fred was embarrassed. He stammered some excuses. "I've really been busy, Father, but I'll get down to confession soon. I'll really be down soon."

At other times, I might have been content to take Fred's promise and then wait for him to show up in church again. But that day something in me led me to take a more direct action. "Oh, no," I said, "I'm not going to let you get away this time. You've got to get your peace right now. Suppose something happens to you today, and you haven't made your peace with God—come on, we can use the patrol car."

Fred's partner took a walk. Fred slid behind the wheel, and I sat in the passenger seat and heard his confession. It was the first time I ever administered the Sacrament of Peace in a Chicago police-department patrol car, but it was not the last.

My unplanned encounter with Fred, and the good that came out of it, led me to be more assertive in similar situations. There were many people in the parish who came to church occasionally, then would disappear for months. If you saw them on the street, they'd act embarrassed and turn the other way. I used to let them go by, but now I found myself actively recruiting them back to church and challenging their indecision: "Why don't you get straightened out with God?" I'd ask a young man.

If he answered that he did not want to, I would ease back and tell him I would be available if he ever wanted to talk with me. The usual answer, however, was something like, "Oh, yes, I want to go to confession with you, Father, but I just don't have the time." When he said that, I had him.

The trick was simple. I was working for God, and I was willing to give road service. As soon as someone said he wanted to but didn't have the time, I'd reply, "We can do it right here, right now, just as we're walking along the sidewalk." And talking softly as we made our way along the crowded sidewalk, I'd hear his confession.

All in all, I heard confessions in such diverse and unexpected places as police patrol cars, public streets, baseball games, bowling alleys, and flophouses.

Once, in a flophouse full of poor derelicts, I ran into a group of desperate characters who wanted to know what I was doing there and who I was working for. I had the impression they were peddling narcotics, but I wasn't sure. As for them, they seemed to think my priestly clothes might be a disguise, maybe I was with a rival narcotics gang, or maybe I was an undercover agent.

"What are you doing here?" one of them asked.

"Taking care of souls."

"Soles? Are you a shoe repairman?"

"No. The kind of souls I'm after never wear out. But sometimes they go in the wrong direction and have to be helped."

"Who are you working for?"

"I'm working for J.C."

"What do you mean, J.C.? What's J.C.? Justice Courts?"

"No, bigger than the courts."

"What's bigger than the courts?"

"My Boss, J.C., is bigger," I said with a smile. "His name is Jesus Christ, 'Superscar'!" *

They laughed and went off about their business.

My encounter with narcotics problems had its humorous side, but in truth those men were agents of the Devil, spreading pain and death. Drug peddlers are particularly evil criminals, for they frequently seek out young people and entice them with free samples. But once a youngster is hooked, the drugs are no longer free—and the new young addict must turn to thievery or prostitution to earn enough money to pay for the drug habit. It is a terrible, painful process, frequently leading to early death.

Drug abuse, much to my chagrin, turned out to be the biggest potential problem among the youth in the parish. The drug peddlers were after them right out in the streets and in the places where adolescent boys like to hang out— places like poolrooms and bowling alleys.

When I saw the situation, I recruited a few charter members and started a teenage club. We fixed up a room in the basement and developed a few programs, but we couldn't draw more than ten or twelve teenagers. The problem was obvious; these kids were being drawn by pool, bowling, jukebox music, places where they could watch television. I knew I couldn't compete for these kids' attention until I had something to draw them to me.

I needed something *visible*—pool tables or television sets, for example—to draw them toward Something *invisible*, namely God. That is the way human psychology works. I knew what had to be done, but we simply didn't have the money to do it.

As my experiences have shown me again and again, the Lord provides, though sometimes His blessings are delivered in the most unexpected ways.

At the same time I was trying to think of ways we could

* When the late Bishop Fulton J. Sheen heard of the musical *Jesus Christ, Superstar,* he remarked, "Jesus Christ was no superstar, he was the Super*scar,* because he suffered for our sins."

raise money to buy the things we needed for our Teen
Club, I also attended to my other duties, one of which
was the Holy Name Society of the parish. One member of
the society—I'll call him Al for the sake of convenience—
impressed me as an unusual man.

He was extremely well dressed in custom-made suits that
were perfectly tailored, though never loud or garish. Despite
his fine clothing, he was an unobtrusive man; he never
raised his voice or argued with the other men. Nevertheless,
all the others seemed to respect him and hold him in high
regard. He looked the natural leader in the group, so I made
him president of the Holy Name Society.

In truth, there was very little for Al to do—the office was
mostly honorary. Nevertheless, from time to time he'd pick
me up in his limousine and as we rode around, we'd discuss the Holy Name Society. He always asked about my
other duties; he seemed to have taken an interest in what
I was trying to do. So I told him about our problems with
the Teen Club.

As I described the scenes on the streets and the drugs and
easy money which tempted young people into lives of crime,
Al listened attentively. But there was no expression on his
face. All he did was nod his head slowly.

When I finished, Al said, "I understand what you need,
Father. I'll see what I can do for you."

I didn't know what Al had in mind or what he could
actually do to help, though he did seem to be successful in a
material sense. Whatever it was that he did for a living, he
appeared to earn a great deal of money from it. But the
fact was, I didn't know what Al did for a living.

Every now and then I'd hear rumors or gossip which con-
nected Al's name to shady involvements, but that was not
unusual. It was rumored that many men in our parish were
mobsters of one sort or another. In any event, I never did
learn with certainty what business Al was in; he himself
mentioned importing and exporting. But whatever it was,
Al was successful at it. He was also a man of his word.

A day or two after our conversation, I was upstairs when I heard someone ring the front doorbell of the parish house. As I started down the stairs, I heard our housekeeper open the door and invite someone in.

From the landing I saw a short, slender man. He wore a black suit and a black hat with a wide brim. Under his jacket he wore a white-on-white shirt and a white necktie. He didn't actually look familiar to me, but I somehow felt I knew him. Then I smiled inwardly as I realized why he reminded me of someone; he looked just like a typical gangster in a Grade-B Hollywood film.

He fidgeted as he stood there and looked around the room, "casing the joint," I believe he would have called it. Each time his eye took in a crucifix or a painting of a holy subject, he seemed to wince.

The housekeeper cleared her throat; our mysterious visitor turned to her and asked, "Is Father DiOrio around?"

I almost laughed out loud at the way he spoke, in an exaggerated tough-guy style, out of one side of his mouth. The other side of his mouth looked as if he wasn't talking at all.

"Yes, Father's in," the housekeeper answered; "who's calling?"

"Louie's the name. Just tell him Al sent me down."

Coming downstairs at that moment, I introduced myself. "Hello, I'm Father DiOrio. May I help you?"

"Well, sort of," he mumbled. "I'm Louie the Bell."

I thought I'd heard him wrong, but it struck me so funny that I laughingly asked, *"Who* are you?"

"Louie the Bell," he repeated with a quick hunch of his shoulders. "Al sent me."

By this time, Louie was getting very nervous. He kept looking at the crosses on the walls, looking around out of the corners of his eyes to see if anyone was watching us or listening to what we were saying. "Can we talk privately in an office?" he asked.

I opened a door, ushered him into an empty office. When I entered behind him, he made me close the door. "I'm gonna tell you things for your ears only."

When I closed the door, Louie quickly glanced around at all the religious artifacts on the walls and shelves. He seemed to shudder. In fact, his body never stopped fidgeting. He had a twitch in his neck and a grimace which pulled his mouth to one side of his face, even when he wasn't talking.

He continued to look around the room, not at me, as he began to speak out of the side of his mouth. "Al says you need some pool tables. That right?"

"Yes," I answered. "We could use a pool table."

He looked around the room again, particularly at the crosses and the holy statues, "Say, Father," he asked with wonderment in his voice, "what are ya gonna do with 'em, anyway?"

I told him I was trying to keep the kids off the streets because the hoodlums were ruining them.

He listened and nodded his head; then with a straight face he told me, "Ya know, Father, I'm all for ya. There's too much crime around. We need guys like you to give us a good society. So I'm gonna try to help you out. Like I said, I'm a friend of Al's. So ya want a couple of pool tables, huh?"

"Well, not a couple," I answered; "they cost a lot of money. I'd be satisfied with one."

"You'll get two," Louie the Bell said out of the side of his mouth. "How about Ping-Pong tables?"

"Two will be excellent," I said.

"You got four. How about a jukebox?"

"Well, I know they're very expensive. Whatever I can get will be fine."

"Uh-uh," he said, shaking his head. "You'll get the best we can give ya. It'll be all chrome with colored lights, and the special feature on this one is when anyone puts a quarter in, it falls into a box that only you can open, and that's good income to keep things movin'—compliments of Al."

I thanked Louie, but when I explained to him that I wanted a jukebox that would play without money, he looked at me as if I were crazy.

When we finished the shopping list of equipment I could use for the Teen Center, my curiosity got the better of me. "Listen," I asked, "why do they call you Louie the Bell?"

Though we were in an office with the door closed, Louie looked around to see if anyone could possibly be listening. Then he sidled right up to me, puffed out his chest with pride, and whispered, "They call me Louie the Bell because when the cops come, I'm the one who rings the bell."

By this time, Louie the Bell looked as if he'd had all the reminders of God he could handle in one session. His fidgeting had increased as time wore on, and the longer we talked the worse it got. It seemed as if each cross on the wall sent out a charge which stung him, or stung his conscience. It was almost laughably obvious that the sooner he could escape from the parish house, the better he would like it.

As I walked him to the front door, Louie seemed to stay as far away as possible from any religious object. On the front walk he turned back, and from beneath the wide brim of his felt hat, he threw me a knowing and friendly wink.

After he left, I laughed to myself at what an odd caricature he was. But he'd been sent by Al, and I knew Al was a resourceful man, so I didn't dismiss Louie the Bell from my mind.

Within a week, all the items Louie had mentioned actually arrived. We got even more than we hoped for. With the help of Louie the Bell, as unexpected a messenger of God's blessings as you could imagine, our Teenage Drop-In Center was successfully launched.

In retrospect, I saw that the entire episode of Louie the Bell contained a clear message—God can and does use anyone to deliver His divine blessings.

During my two years at Holy Guardian Angel, hundreds of youngsters frequented the Teen Center. There is no doubt in my mind that most of them were initially attracted by the material equipment—the pool tables, the TV set, and the jukebox. But it is equally certain that many of them became actively involved in the life of the church.

There is no way to measure *how much good* was done for these young people, but it is certain that *good was done*. Not only was good done, it was helped along by such unlikely characters as Al and Louie the Bell. Surely, the ways of the Lord are mysterious.

Six

THE SEEDS
OF CHANGE

After two years of energetic service in Holy Guardian Angel parish, the joys of that apostolate came to an end as the unknown promise of another began. I was assigned to Our Lady of Pompeii Church, relatively nearby.

Our Lady of Pompeii, in fact, was an outgrowth from Holy Guardian Angel parish. As the population of the area became more predominantly Italo-American, and as the Italo-Americans extended their neighborhoods, another church was needed. Our Lady of Pompeii was situated next door to the famed St. Frances Cabrini Hospital, named after Mother Cabrini.

It was an interesting coincidence that I, a Scalabrini Father, was stationed next door to a hospital named to commemorate the saintly work of Mother Cabrini. The co-incidence is in the historical fact that on the occasion of her first apostolic venture in behalf of Italian immigrants in North America, it was the founder of our congregation, Bishop John Baptist Scalabrini, who had blessed Mother Cabrini's undertaking and bestowed the missionary cross upon her.

A short time after I arrived at Our Lady of Pompeii, the nearness of Mother Cabrini Hospital helped to save my life. How that came about, and the consequences it had for the future growth of my priesthood, were all part of God's plan.

My work at Our Lady of Pompeii included retreats, hospital work, and other parish duties, thus widening the range of my experience. But youth work held a special place in my attention. I have always been drawn to youth work, even to this day. And my regard for young people seems to be reciprocal; they seek me as I seek them.

The lesson I've drawn from my work with young people is uplifting; namely, we are all students, even the oldest among us, just as we are all teachers, even the youngest. If the young people with whom I've come in contact have learned half as much from me as I have learned from them, then we all have grown by our experience.

The Italo-American neighborhoods of Chicago, and the styles of the people who lived in them, were familiar to me. As soon as I arrived at Our Lady of Pompeii, I set about making contact with the kids on the streets, most of whom had little or no previous contact with the church. I approached them as a friend, and the kids accepted me in the same spirit. Before long, fifty or sixty of them were involved in the life of the church as altar boys through their involvement in the Boys' Club.

At the back of my mind, where they had rested for years, were my doubts about my own vocation—was I truly meant to be a Scalabrini Father? Is that what God intended for me? Or was His plan the same as my half-conscious desire to have a universal ministry, in which I could bring His love to all mankind?

These questions were always with me, but they did not prevent me from throwing myself into my priestly work with all my energy and dedication. My work among the immigrant teenagers was going so well that I began to wonder if this *was* what God wanted my priesthood to be. I was feeling a sense of growth and fulfillment, a sense that I was becoming a stronger priest, when suddenly sickness struck.

With no warning, I had a sudden recurrence of my intestinal problem and began to hemorrhage severely. They rushed me next door to Mother Cabrini Hospital, where I underwent immediate surgery.

The bleeding was stopped, but for a day or two following the operation, it was not certain that I'd survive. In fact, the word was passed to the youngsters that I might be dying.

As I learned later, all fifty or sixty of them wanted to visit me in the hospital; they were afraid that I, their priest, was going to die.

But they all couldn't come into the hospital; there were too many of them. In fact, kids were not allowed to visit patients at all, so some nuns sneaked a few kids into my room. They sat on my bed. "You gonna get better, Father Ralph?" they asked. "Please, we want you back!" I was so moved by their love for me that tears came into my eyes. I blessed them and they left.

A few minutes later, I heard a large group of voices outside my window. I was on the second floor and could hear these voices through the closed windows, coming up the stairs from outside the hospital. I pulled myself out of bed, worked my way to the window, and looked down. There on the lawn under my window was the whole group of my altar boys, saying the rosary for me.

It was one of the most moving moments of my life. I waved to them and blessed them all. I was really crying as I made my way back to bed. And then I got better. After that, I got the Healing. What a marvelous example of intercessory prayer!

During my stay in the hospital, I became quite friendly with the late Dr. Carmen Pintozzi, the man who had performed the surgery on me. The doctor had a reputation both for his medical skill and his warm compassion. If he prescribed a medicine and found that the patient couldn't afford it, he'd pay for it himself. It was widely known that Dr. Pintozzi was a devout and dedicated man, committed to working for the good of the people.

Day after day, whether he had to see me medically or not, this marvelous man would take time from his rounds to visit me. He'd pull up a chair, and we'd talk. Actually, he'd do much of the talking and I much of the listening.

He talked about many things, but he was particularly interested in discussing the similarities between his calling and mine. He pointed out to me that the practice of medicine is a combination of science and art, of the material and the spiritual.

Doctors cannot cure every illness. And furthermore, even when they apparently do effect a cure, often they themselves cannot fully explain why.

Dr. Pintozzi's discussions about the great mysteries of sickness and healing gave me fresh cause for reflection, for his words and my own illness had reawakened in me my childhood thoughts about a career in one of the health professions.

Perhaps, I wondered, there is still a chance to combine my priesthood with my old aspiration to help cure illness and suffering. My thoughts, however, went no further. I had no idea what form such a turn of events might take.

Seventeen years later, however, that form was revealed to me in the single, most startling moment of my life—the moment when it became transparently clear that God had blessed me with the charism of healing, that God had chosen me to be a channel for His Grace.

❖

After I left the hospital, I recuperated slowly. In light of the fact that the duties I was called upon to perform in Our Lady of Pompeii were extremely demanding, my superior decided to transfer me. I was assigned to Mother Cabrini parish, where my share of parish duties could be kept light until I'd recuperated.

I was overjoyed at my new assignment; Mother Cabrini was the parish in which I'd been ordained. Returning there four years later served as a benchmark. I could take stock of where I'd been over the first years of my priesthood.

The first time I returned to St. Frances Mother Cabrini Church, I stood in the back. There were no people in the church, but it was not empty. I could almost see the Bishop's hand as it approached my head to anoint me with the holy oil; I could almost hear his deep voice as he intoned, "You are a priest forever!"

My parish duties were quite varied, though not as rigorous

as they'd been at Our Lady of Pompeii. My opportunities for serving included teaching, youth retreat work, a hospital chaplaincy, parish renewal weekends, and lecturing. Added to this was the great opportunity to do postgraduate study at the Dominican House of Studies in Oak Park, Illinois, where I studied spiritual and ascetic theology. I also attended courses in psychology and ethics.

In addition, at the Dominican House of Studies I had the exceptional privilege of receiving spiritual and intellectual guidance from Father Sebastian Carlson. I also continued to receive confessional guidance from another Dominican, Father John Gaines, who had been my spiritual director during the four years of theology prior to my being ordained. Both these men had decisive effects on my life, for they redirected the course of my priesthood and pointed me toward my current vocation as a diocesan priest.

✣

The parish, and most of Chicago, for that matter, was undergoing great social change; what had been an almost totally Italo-American area was now a melting pot, one of those social stews for which America is so famous. There were Germans, Poles, Irish, and Eastern Europeans. There were still more Italo-Americans in the area than any other single ethnic group, but they were not the majority, and their numbers were shrinking. As they moved out, perhaps a step up in material terms, other people took their places in the never-ending social mobility of American life.

This time most of the new people in the neighborhood were Spanish-speaking, mainly Puerto Ricans, but there were some Mexicans too.

To help us in our work with our Hispanic parishioners, the Archdiocese of Chicago sponsored courses in the Spanish language and culture, of which I availed myself.

The last group to enter the area were the blacks, some of whom came directly from the South.

The social pressures built up by these changes were great, and each group had to cope with its own problems. But the

Spanish-speaking always had the additional problem of language. As I was assigned to work with our Spanish-speaking parishioners, it made good sense for me to learn their language.

Learning Spanish had a twofold result. In the first instance, it prepared me to serve my Spanish-speaking parishioners. In the second, which took place several years later, it served as a direct link leading to my current work in the Healing Ministry. In retrospect, I see that the events of my life have not followed one upon the other by coincidence or chance. They are, each and every one of them, pieces of God's divine plan.

My work among the Spanish-speaking people threw me into contact with a new, rich, and complex culture. Not only did I have to learn a language, but a new set of customs, manners, and ways of communication.

Intellectually and emotionally it was a very stimulating time of my life. I enjoyed the challenge and the new things I was learning. But the very broadness of the experience brought home to me again how narrow my Scalabrini missionary priesthood seemed. I felt a calling to bring God to everyone, but my congregation was only geared to Italian immigrants and, by chance, to Hispanic newcomers. At times I felt myself straining against these limitations, but I took no action. I kept my doubts to myself.

Finally I raised the question with Father Sebastian. He helped me to clarify the issues and agreed with my feeling that the Scalabrini congregation was not the place I could best serve the Church. He thought I ought to join the Dominican order, but I never seriously considered the idea. I knew I would only leave the Scalabrinians to become a diocesan priest. That was my goal if I decided to change.

But the decision did not come quickly or easily. Priestly responsibilities are too great for superficial answers or snap judgments. One must examine the issues thoroughly and be certain of one's true desire before making such a serious move as seeking a change in religious status.

I had to be certain, but I also had to be honest with God and myself. Once I'd ascertained the rightness of my conscience, I had to follow it. If it became clear to me that this was what God wanted, then, notwithstanding pain, embarrassment, or sacrifice, I would have to go ahead and do it. I would have to step out, with faith in God, whatever the dangers.

As a result of discussions with Father Sebastian and my own inner monologue, I came to the following understanding: my doubts about continuing as a Scalabrini Father had raised what was essentially a moral issue. I had to heed my conscience and follow its lead. If it led to change, then I would formally seek exclaustration from the Missionary Father of St. Charles for the purpose of becoming a diocesan priest.

Now that I was clearer about my situation, I discussed it with fellow priests, trying to gather advice and other opinions. The word that I was once again thinking about leaving the congregation must have gotten around. A short time later I received an unexpected phone call from my superior. He got right to the point. "Ralph, we have a problem in Atikokan, Canada. One of our priests has come back ill. Would you mind going?"

He didn't have to ask my consent, I would have had to go whether I agreed or not. But perhaps he was subtly testing my attitude, to see if I'd be at all reluctant, or if I'd reveal any desire to leave the congregation.

I thought quickly: if God wants me to leave this congregation, God will lead me from it. Then I thought: I should give the congregation another chance or give myself another chance with it. Maybe this *is* what God wants me to do, and I haven't understood Him yet.

So I took a deep breath and answered, "Of course not, Father. When do I leave?" With those words, I submitted to authority and unreservedly accepted my assignment to the Canadian missions.

Seven

MOMENT
OF DECISION

When I was ready to go north, an old classmate of mine, Father Al Corridin who had been four or five years ahead of me, showed up. Father Al was the vocational director for the Scalabrini congregation in the Western Province. His duties required a lot of traveling; as it happened, he was on his way to Duluth, Minnesota, so I took a ride with him.

It was my first visit to Duluth, and it came about by chance. Or did it? Many years later, I returned to Duluth on an annual basis to direct crusades for the Charismatic Renewal and to lead Healing services.

When Father Al dropped me off, I was met by Father Julio Gragniani, God rest his soul, the pastor at Atikokan. He had driven down to get me, and we continued the trip north.

It was my first visit to Canada, and the natural beauty of the landscape overwhelmed me. I am a great admirer of man- or woman-made art, but the greatest artist is God Himself, the ultimate Author of all beauty.

The month was September, and the foliage of the wide Canadian countryside flared with the brilliant hues of fire and flame. Between the areas of woodland, we drove through seemingly endless wide-open spaces. I began to sense the remoteness of the place to which I was going. My imagination responded to the image of the missionary priest who had done God's work along the frontiers of civilization. The emptier and more remote the landscape grew, the more I looked forward to arriving in Atikokan to begin my new apostolate.

Atikokan is a small mining town in Ontario, Canada. When I arrived in 1961, the population was a rich mixture of French, Germans, Poles, Ukranians, local Canadian Indians, and, of course, Italian immigrants. Almost everyone worked for the Steep Rock or Kalen Iron Ore Mines.

The town was remote and isolated; the nearest city, Port Arthur, was 125 miles away. There was a railroad track, but the train wasn't running. That was why Father Julio had driven down to Duluth to get me.

A few days after I arrived, I received a letter from one of my comical cousins: "Dear Ralph," he wrote, "I looked on the map to see where they sent you. When I finally found the spot, all I could wonder was—what did Cousin Ralph do wrong?"

Of course, I hadn't done anything wrong. All I'd done was to question openly my role as a Scalabrini Father. My assignment to Atikokan might have looked suspicious, and my cousin, for one, assumed it was some kind of punishment. But I never actually knew if I was being punished, and so I gave my superiors the benefit of the doubt and went about the work of performing my duties as well as I could.

As soon as I got to know the people, I relaxed. Any apprehension I might have had disappeared. They were clearly my kind of people, perhaps a bit on the rough-and-ready side, but honest, down-to-earth, and, for the most part, God-loving.

There were five Protestant churches and our Scalabrini mission, the only Catholic church in the area. In view of the limited possibilities in the area, the Protestant ministers and we Catholic priests drew on each other in a way and to a degree that would have been thought unusual almost anyplace else.

In our common Christian work we helped each other, often sharing resources and car-pooling long before the idea became popular in the States.

Since I'd entered the seminary at fifteen, I'd had little

opportunity for prolonged contact with Protestants. Now I suddenly found myself working closely with Protestant clergymen, whom I immediately discovered were my colleagues. As I got to know my Protestant brothers better, I learned to love them, and to love the Protestant churches too.

These events happened at a time when the concept of ecumenism was just beginning to be heard. It seems as if God placed me in that situation so he could continue to prepare me for my present service in the Healing Ministry. It was another reminder that God, in His Divine Providence, has been preparing me for the Healing Ministry from the moment of my conception.

My life was being filled in like a mosaic into which the Lord placed a new piece from time to time.

❖

As my Canadian assignment drew to a close, I was about to complete the fifth year of my priesthood and enter the sixth. The Scalabrini congregation observed a tradition called *Aggiornamento*; it was their custom to send priests to Rome for a year of study every sixth year. These postgraduate courses were given at the famous Gregorian University in Rome.

After receiving formal notice that I would participate in *Aggiornamento*, I began to prepare. I was looking forward to seeing my classmates in Rome, and to a full year of study and reflection, when a second communication arrived.

My orders had been changed. Instead of joining my classmates in the *Aggiornamento*, I was to report to a seminary in Cornwall, New York, and assume the position of Assistant Novice Master.

I was disappointed, for I had deeply wanted to have that year of study in Rome. It has been part of my lifelong dream, a dream that has yet to be fulfilled. But another part of me felt differently. This new assignment would be a challenging one. It would give me the opportunity to exercise my natural inclinations to lead an ascetic life and to work with young people. As a teacher, I immediately en-

My maternal grandparents, Nonno Betto and Nonna Crocifissa.

My father and I. When this picture was taken, in 1951, I was twenty-one and in the sixth year of my training to become a priest. My father was hard at work in his stonecutting business.

A family portrait from 1955. My brother Louis, father, mother, and my sister Jude Ann.

"Thou Art a Priest Forever." This is the moment of my ordination, on June 1, 1957. The late Bishop Raymond J. Hillinger lays his hands on my head and ordains me into the Roman Catholic priesthood.

A few moments after my ordination, I bestow my first blessing on my mother. My second blessing was for my father.

Prior to a Healing Service, I prepare by private and contempla-
tive prayer.

At the start of a service, I frequently try to relax the people and put them at ease with a humorous word or two.

As the service proceeds, God takes charge and Ralph DiOrio grows less present. Here I have entered a trancelike state and am in the act of calling a Healing.

I am a two-way channel. God's love for His people flows through me in one direction, and their love for Him flows in the other.

Often I will feel an energy go through me, an energy of knowledge, which causes me to say to a particular man or woman, "You have arthritis [or another problem] and you are going to be healed!"

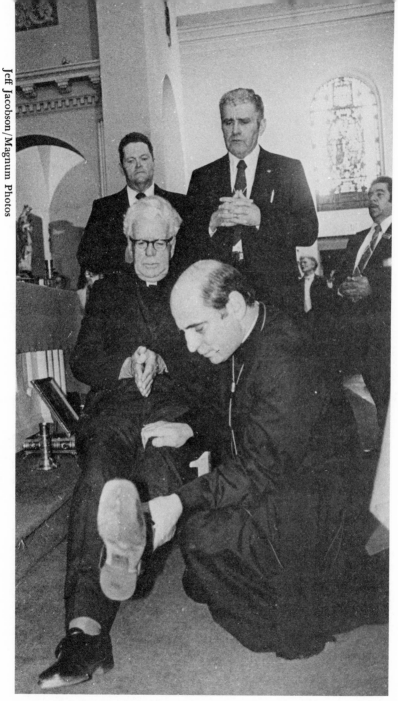

Men and women of the Church frequently attend our services.

When this photo was taken in 1980, Leo Perras had been out of his wheelchair for almost two years after having been confined to it for twenty-one years. (See Chapter 15)

A three-year-old girl who was healed of blindness.

After a powerful and intense service, my mother and I stand before the altar, exhausted but still smiling.

Here I am in my office, where the phone seems to ring continuously.

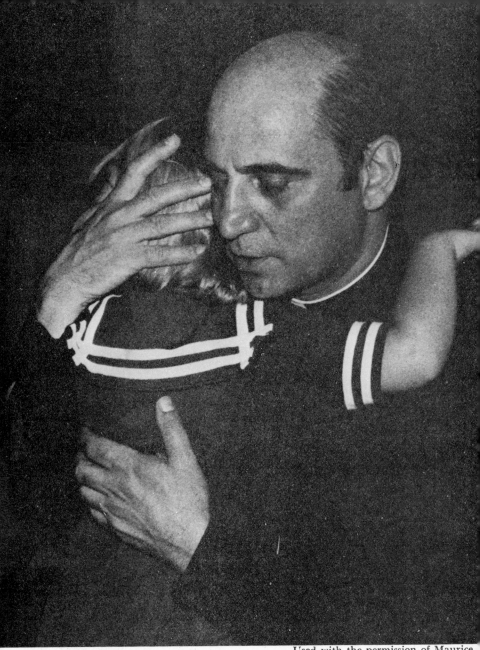

My heart breaks most when I pray over a child with no apparent result. This child had no special need, so I blessed her with the Love of Jesus.

visioned this new assignment as an opportunity to provide intellectual, moral, and spiritual guidance to young aspirants to the priesthood.

I absorbed my disappointment and went to Cornwall, looking forward to my new duties.

My assignment in Cornwall did not disappoint me. The duties of Assistant Novice Master suited my temperament and were personally rewarding. While in Cornwall, I taught religion and philosophy at the Storm King Military Academy and came into frequent contact with the West Point community.

But beyond these activities, and in some ways of more significance, once again I found myself in frequent contact with Protestant clergymen. Our cooperative projects and lengthy dialogues were mutually enriching. This involvement with my Protestant brothers was intellectually and spiritually invigorating. The spirit of ecumenism was beginning to fill the entire Christian world with a new energy. The immortal words of Pope John XXIII echoed everywhere with his call for the renewal of the life of the Church and for the growth of Christian unity.

John's call for a "new Pentecost" ignited a new fire of zeal in my life in the Church. His words breathed a spirit of new life into the vocations of countless priests, myself included. His words thrust us headlong into the Ecumenical Movement.

As the spirit of ecumenism began its surge through the entire Christian world, I saw that once again I was in the right place at the right time, enacting in my own cooperation with Protestants the new message Pope John XXIII had given the world. Once again, the Lord was preparing me, this time for the ecumenical spirit which would shape my eventual role in the Healing Ministry.

In my mind, ecumenism meant that Christians should no longer be *divided* by denominations, but rather should interact as brethren. John's proclamation confirmed my own heart's desire for the universal togetherness of all God's children. The fact that this confirmation had come from the head of the Church gave my feelings an additional lift. With faith and joy, I launched myself into the mighty river of the Ecumenical Movement, intent on doing my share to reach the goal described by Pope John.

Growth, no matter how natural and healthy it may be, is often accompanied by growing pains. In my case, the pains had to do with the old problem of my limited role as a Scalabrini Father. Tasting the new wine of ecumenism only served to strengthen my desire for a more universal priesthood. In fact, my participation in the Ecumenical Movement finally removed my doubts and clarified my position.

Once and for all, I understood that the Scalabrini congregation was not for me. The decision I reached after long years of doubt and perplexity was a personal decision. I meant no criticism of the Scalabrini congregation or of its compassionate aims. I respected the congregation, and I continue to. All I meant to express by my decision were my individual and personal goals. In short, the Scalabrini congregation was not the place for me, personally. It was not a place in which I could fulfill the universal role for which God was preparing me.

After years of painful soul-searching, I was certain. Then and only then did I take action on this decision. I began the process of seeking exclaustration, the canonical technical name for the formal permission to withdraw from a specific commitment in order to enter another. In my case, I sought formal permission to withdraw from my religious status and obedience to the Scalabrini missionary congregation in order to enter into a new status and obedience as a diocesan priest.

When my Scalabrini superiors received my request, they tried to ignore it. They responded by reassigning me. This time they sent me as a temporary pastor to the Scalabrini mission in Cincinnati, Ohio.

Perhaps my superiors thought I'd drop my case for transfer while I was in Cincinnati, but I didn't. I was resolute, and I had the added support of knowing that I was not alone in my attitude.

I was not the only priest in our congregation who was questioning his vocation; many of the other Americans were suffering the same doubts. Some of them even abandoned the priesthood altogether. But that solution never occurred to me. I loved being a priest, and I have always loved being a priest. I was a good priest, and I wanted to continue being a good priest. I only wanted to change the *type* of priest I was. So I went about the whole process of changing my status in the prescribed canonical manner. While in Cincinnati, I reiterated my request for exclaustration.

These precise and formal steps on my part posed another kind of problem for my superiors. If I left their congregation by going through the proper chain of command and the correct Church authority, it would mean that other Scala-brini Fathers who wanted to leave the congregation could do so without having to face the terrible thought of quitting the priesthood as their only way out of an untenable situation. I think my superiors felt that if I were allowed to leave, the floodgates would open and their congregation would lose a lot of priests. Therefore they treated my request with great caution and slow deliberation. So slow, in fact, that they hardly acknowledged it at all.

But they did respond in an indirect way. After a short stay in the Midwest during which my resolve did not falter, my superiors moved me to the East. They seemed to have felt that if they brought me closer to my family, I would change my mind about wanting to leave the congregation. I didn't. My new assignment was in St. Anthony's parish in New Haven, Connecticut, but the change in location did nothing to change my mind. I persisted in my decision to follow my conscience.

Following the pattern of my career, my stay at St. Anthony's was brief. But as a result of that assignment, I made contact with many people who remembered me years later and came to attend our Healing Services. Some even joined our Healing Ministry.

During my few months in New Haven, I immersed myself in the duties of the parish, but I continued to reiterate the call of my conscience. In response to this call, my superiors, for their own reasons, sent me to the Provincial House in Greenwich Village, New York.

In Greenwich Village I spent six intensive months, mostly working on the streets with beatniks and drug addicts as a sort of "junkie priest." In addition to these extraordinary duties, I also maintained my regular pastoral duties.

My experiences were growing richer and more varied. All the different kinds of things I'd done in my life and, more particularly, in my priesthood seemed to be adding up.

All the pieces seemed to be settling into a specific design, though I couldn't see it clearly yet. So I did as I've always done; I simply submitted to God's will and sought wise counsel wherever I could find it.

✣

The oldest priest in the Greenwich Village Provincial House, Our Lady of Pompeii, on Carmine Street near Sixth Avenue, was Father Giuseppe Rizzi, an eighty-year-old retired Scalabrinian. Father Rizzi's hearing was poor, but he took great pleasure in watching television with the sound turned off. He was a very calm man who did not waste his words. He seemed to me to be both prudent and wise, so I told him the story of my intent to transfer from the Scalabrini congregation, a congregation of which he himself had been a member for the better part of sixty years.

Father Rizzi turned up his hearing aid and watched my face intently as I told my story. When I finished, Father Rizzi took a pinch of snuff in each nostril, sneezed mightily, and finally said, pointing his index finger at me all the while, "If God wants you to be a secular priest, nobody on earth will stop it!"

Then he turned down his hearing aid and returned his gaze to the television set.

✤

After six months in Greenwich Village, the newly elected Provincial assigned me to Utica, in upstate New York. As for my repeated requests for exclaustration, he got right to the point. He let me know that he didn't want to hear another word about it.

Short of committing an act of insubordination, all I could do was comply with my new orders. I was under the obligation of holy obedience to the Provincial, so I submitted. But Father Rizzi's words of wisdom gave me added hope; perhaps God's will was being expressed through the actions of the Provincial. Perhaps this new assignment would lead me closer to my heart's desire. So I went to Utica and remained there for three productive years.

I taught at St. Peter's High School, and after a while I started my own radio program for the sick and the shut-ins. It was a half-hour show, all of it in Italian. I called it *L'Ora Catolica,* the Catholic Hour. Maybe the most interesting aspect of this program, in terms of my own life, was that it was directed at sick people who could not come to church. This was when the sick began to draw my attention irresistibly.

✤

In January 1966, my father fell seriously ill. When I received the news, I immediately phoned the Scalabrinian offices and requested an emergency leave so I could return to Providence for a day or two to see my father. But the Provincial Superior was away, and the substituting Superior claimed he did not have the authority to grant my request.

Responding directly from my heart and conscience, I told the substitute Superior that common decency and the natural bond of love between a son and his father warranted— even demanded—that he grant me permission to attend to my father.

Apparently I argued my case well, or touched the man's compassion, for the substitute Superior finally granted my request. I immediately returned to Providence, where I spent three days at my father's beside in St. Joseph's Hospital.

As it turned out, those three days were extremely important. My father and I had the opportunity to reacquaint ourselves with each other and come to a mature and loving understanding. My presence was a great and sustaining consolation to him. In six months' time, my father would die.

❖

A few months later, back in Utica, I got a phone call from my mother late one night. She told me my grandfather had passed away. It was not completely unexpected news because my grandfather was ninety-six years old. But I had been very close to him, especially as a child, and the memories of that loving relationship have always stayed with me. So I was sad when I learned that my Nonno Betto was dead, and I wanted to go home to celebrate his funeral mass.

But the Scalabrini rules were very strict; we were not allowed to go home, even when a relative died. So my superiors refused to let me go home for my grandfather's funeral. The pain I experienced was profound; it went to the very core of my being. My beloved Nonno Betto was no more, and I had not even been allowed to attend his funeral. All I could do was to go to our chapel and pray. As I prayed, I saw through a veil of tears a thousand happy and loving moments I had spent with my grandfather. From that moment there was no doubt or any room for further procrastination. I would leave the congregation of the Scalabrini Fathers.

The arbitrary refusal to let me attend my grandfather's funeral clarified my mind and completely focused my intentions. I repeated my request for a transfer, but the Superior General refused again. This time, however, I was fully prepared to take the action I had held back from on previous occasions. I wrote and presented my case to the Apostolic Delegate. The Apostolic Delegate, in turn, telephoned the General, who happened to be visiting the United

States, and told him to grant me a year's leave of absence.

A leave of absence represented progress in my case, but it was not the perfect solution. I'd have time to think and take steps for the future, but my status was not clearly defined. Though I was on leave from my normal duties, I had not been formally released from my vows of obedience to my Scalabrini superiors. That meant I was not yet free to petition a Bishop of my choice for acceptance into his diocese as a diocesan priest.

My superiors avoided the issue of my status by simply refusing to give me any written document at all. But they did give me $200, and with that amount of money in my pocket I left Utica and headed home to Providence and into another ordeal. God was about to break me so that He could raise me up once again.

Eight

~~~~~~

DIVINELY BROKEN,
DIVINELY RAISED

I returned to Providence at the beginning of July. One Sunday morning two weeks later—it was July 16, to be exact—my mother, brother Louis, and I returned from church to discover my father slumped over in a chair, unconscious.

Louis and I carefully carried him up to his bed. I anointed my father and tried to revive him. As I touched him with the sacred oil, he awoke and asked in a feeble voice, "What happened, son?"

I told him everything was going to be all right, but when I mentioned that the ambulance was on the way, he cried out, "No! No! I don't want the ambulance!" The ambulance came. As they carried him out on the stretcher, he was crying, "I don't want to go! I love you, Molly! I want you, Molly! I love you!" Molly is my mother.

He was carried, helpless, from the master bedroom, through the parlor, and out the front door. Mom accompanied him in the ambulance to St. Joseph's Hospital. She told us later that he held her hand the whole way.

I stayed with my father in his hospital room from twelve noon to ten minutes before six, but he never came out of his coma again. Intermittently, I prayed for him all afternoon.

A few times I stood by the window looking out, but my eyes were not seeing what was out there. In my mind I was reliving many scenes from the past between my father and me, good times and bad times. I remembered the time he took me for an ice-cream cone and a photograph on the way home from church when I was a little boy. I remembered how big and hard his hands, roughened from years of hard labor, seemed to me when I was little.

The reflections which passed through my mind touched on numerous things. I recalled how hard he had worked all his life and thought about his life in general, and this train of thought led to the inescapable knowledge that everyone must die. Then my eyes returned to the still form of my father on the white hospital bed, and I resumed the recitation of the prayers for the dying and the dead.

At ten of six, I walked out to go to the lavatory. My mother went in. When I came back five minutes later, my mother came out of the room and said, "Daddy just passed away."

My mother had always said that she would be with my father at the moment he died and that he would just hold her. Her whole life, she said, was to save my father's soul. That was the gift God gave to her, that she should be a good wife. And it was my father's blessing. As the Scriptures say, "Blessed is the man who has a good wife."

Three days later, on July 19, my thirty-seventh birthday, I said the mass for my father's funeral.

✤

After I left home to enter the seminary in 1945, my father went ahead with his plans without me. He started his own small stonecutting and sandblasting business. He and my mother worked hard together; she kept the books and took care of the office. When they acquired enough savings, they bought a small house. His business survived, but my father never got rich. When he took sick, the family finances were in trouble.

My father died of asphyxiation. He had emphysema and other respiratory complications. Years of hard labor as a stonecutter had exposed him to silicone dust, which he had inhaled in fatal quantities. He also had indulged heavily in cigarette smoking. The nature of his final illness was such that it kept him home as an invalid for an extended period. When I arrived home, my father had not been working for six months, and the bills were beginning to pile up.

For the next nine months, my energies were divided among sustaining myself as a priest, obtaining my release from the Scalabrini congregation, and trying to earn enough money to take care of my mother's house and put food on the table for my mother and me.

I sustained myself as a priest by celebrating mass each day at various diocesan and Scalabrini parishes. For a while, daily stipends for mass celebration were my sole form of income, which came to approximately twenty-five dollars a week. It was hardly enough money to support my mother and me and pay the mortgage payments on her house.

As the situation grew more desperate, I broadened my scope. I took on handyman-type work—some house painting, some small carpentry jobs.

When they learned of my situation, a few friends and relatives who knew of my art work asked me to do paintings or drawings for them. I've never had the time to develop my interest in art fully, but when the opportunity arose, I took courses. When I was stationed in Cincinnati, I studied painting and drawing at the Gebhart School of Art. During my years in Utica, I studied privately with a professional artist.

I gladly accepted these commissions and fulfilled them with watercolor or pastel portraits.

Word of my paintings got around. Two sympathetic diocesan pastors in Providence, Monsignor Cavallaro of Mt. Carmel Church and Father Madden of St. Anthony's parish, invited me to paint church designs and decorations. This provided me with additional income.

The good pastors' interest, in addition to helping me earn some money, was to help me stay close to the Church. They knew of my situation with my congregation, and they responded with solidarity and support.

Support came from others also. The then Chancellor of Providence, Daniel Riley, now Bishop Riley of Norwich, Connecticut, was a strong source of guidance and direction during those months of ordeal in Providence.

Through the support of these good priests and others, God sustained me. I remained on the right track, but not without some close calls.

At times, the necessity to earn a living for my mother and me almost drove me to desperation. Since I never entertained thoughts of leaving the priesthood, the occupations I could consider were quite limited. Then I heard the story of one of my Scalabrini contemporaries who also desired to leave the congregation, but not the priesthood. His solution to the problem, after receiving permission, was to join the Navy as a chaplain. His solution seemed so reasonable that I acted on an immediate impulse and followed his example; I volunteered to join the Navy as a chaplain.

After I passed a variety of examinations, the Navy offered me a commission as a first lieutenant, the equivalent of a captain in the Army. The salary accompanying this position would have allowed me to support my mother while retaining and sustaining my priesthood as a chaplain, so I was prepared to accept the Navy's offer. All that was needed was one document, the official proof that I was, in fact, a properly ordained priest.

I wrote to my Scalabrini superiors and requested a copy of the required document. But they did not respond. They never said they were refusing; it was just that the document never arrived. And since they never informed me that they were refusing, I believed the document would eventually arrive and I waited. This waiting period grew so long that I missed the time limit set by the Navy.

While it was happening, my attempt to join the Navy was a matter of great concern to me. I grew impatient with my superiors for their long delay. But later, as my life unfolded, I understood that the Lord was acting through my superiors when He caused them to hold back my certificate of ordination; it was simply not in His plan to let me join the Navy.

To become a Navy chaplain had appeared to be a good solution. In fact, it seemed to be the only solution. When I learned that my application deadline had passed, my spirits sank. I felt broken and wondered if the Lord had forgotten me.

In some ways, this was the low point of my priesthood and my life. I felt an immense but unknown energy within me, an energy to do the Lord's work, but I felt powerless to use it. My unclear status with the Scalabrini congregation hung on me like a chain, and I could not understand what I had done to be so broken and so lost.

In my perplexity I prayed to God for guidance, for a sign, for a direction which would lead me out of my confusion and into the flower'ng of my priesthood. As if in answer to my earnest prayers, I received a visit from Father Joseph Invernizzi. Father Joe was a fellow Scalabrini, but he was an older man, more familiar with the ways of the Scalabrini hierarchy.

Though he himself had no intention of leaving the congregation, he'd taken a special interest in my case and so he had looked into it. His visit was for the purpose of telling me what he had learned. He got right to the point. My superiors in the congregation were set on blocking my request for exclaustration and were prepared to block me as long as I maintained my position.

Father Joe, indignant at the way I was being treated, gave me some advice. I trusted him and did as he said, which was to seek help directly from the Pope's office.

Finally, after a long struggle in which I tried to follow established procedures, I had recourse to Rome. I wrote to the Consistorial Congregation, then under the leadership of Cardinal Confalonieri, telling my story and presenting my case.

As part of their procedure, the staff of the Consistorial

Congregation examined my official dossier, which included all the reports I'd ever received since entering the seminary. When they found no evidence of disobedience or disciplinary problems of any kind, they concluded that the basis for my request was a legitimate attempt to rectify the status of my priestly vocation for reasons of my conscience.

They understood the nature of my position, namely that I was trying to follow my conscience and become a diocesan priest so I could serve the Church more universally.

When my case had been thoroughly examined, the Consistorial Congregation informed me that my request for a change in status was perfectly valid. They also disclosed that my superiors were still blocking my transfer.

At this point, I began to feel trapped in a situation that had no logic to it. On the one hand, Rome agreed with my position, but on the other, nobody seemed willing to do anything about it, anything that could force the issue and compel the Scalabrinis to release me.

During this ordeal, Father Invernezzi and Father Ruba, a Dominican priest at Providence College and my confessor in Providence, continued to support me with their deep concern and guidance. They cautioned me against despairing of the situation and counseled patience. With their encouragement, I reopened my correspondence with Rome.

This time I stated my case as clearly and firmly as I possibly could. But I made no threats or accusations. I merely stated the situation as I perceived it and trusted in the Lord.

Two weeks later I received official notification that I was released from my oath of obedience to the Scalabrini congregation, the Missionary Order of St. Charles. Released. It was 1968. I had served eleven years as a Scalabrini missionary priest. With a sudden rush of enthusiasm, I eagerly looked forward to a new phase in my priesthood.

Nine

A DIOCESAN
PRIEST AT LAST

A year earlier, when I was ministering in Utica, I followed the advice of my confessor, Father Mahoney, the pastor of St. Anthony's parish in Utica, and directed a preliminary application for acceptance to Bishop Bernard J. Flanagan of the diocese of Worcester, Massachusetts.

Bishop Flanagan granted me an interview, and on May 9, 1967, I traveled to Worcester, Massachusetts. This date seems to hold special significance for me; nine years later, on May 9, 1976, the healing powers of the Lord broke through and began to manifest themselves through me.

Sitting in the waiting room of the Chancery of the Worcester diocese, I thought over my situation, particularly my need to be accepted into a diocese, and I wondered what Bishop Flanagan would be like. The first glimpse I got of this man, a man who was to play such a central role in my life and priesthood, set my fears to rest.

As I wrote earlier, during my childhood I'd been an avid movie fan. One of my favorites was Spencer Tracy, especially in his classic portrayal of the great Father Flanagan in the film, *Boys' Town*.

When Bishop Flanagan stepped into the waiting room to take me into his office, I was astonished to see how closely he resembled Spencer Tracy. In fact, he looked just like him.

This physical resemblance to one of my childhood favorites was, of course, reassuring. But I soon learned that the resemblance between the Bishop and the actor went beyond their looks and the coincidence of names; Tracy played Father Flanagan in the movie. For me, as for millions of

146

other Americans, Spencer Tracy was the very image of a man of warmth, gentility, understanding, dependability, and, perhaps above all, a man of character. Bishop Bernard J. Flanagan, in real life, is no less a man.

The results of my interview with Bishop Flanagan were positive and auspicious; he accepted me into his diocese, but on the condition that my transfer was carried out according to proper canonical procedures.

As matters turned out, the Bishop's stipulation was met in less than a year. I returned to Worcester on March 29, 1968, in my new role as a diocesan priest. I have been ministering in the Worcester Diocese since that time, though my official incardination did not take place until March 19, 1972.

My expectations were borne out from the start. As a diocesan priest, I more clearly experienced the joys of my priesthood, for now I had the liberty to be as God meant me to be. In this mood of renewed vigor, I threw myself into my new diocesan duties.

For my first assignment, Bishop Flanagan sent me to St. Anne's Parish in Leominster, Massachusetts, where I served for two years. I ministered to the sick, worked with teenagers, and taught in several parish education programs. I also had the good fortune to introduce the Christian Family Movement (CFM) into that parish, where it took strong root and continues to thrive.

While at St. Anne's, I followed the suggestion of a psychologist I'd met and took some postgraduate classes in psychology. This psychologist thought the courses would enhance my effectiveness as a priest by helping me to assimilate the various elements of my training. Later, I saw that the classes, which I attended with great interest, were an early step in my attempt to develop a holistic ministry.

Around this time, another significant agent of growth and development entered my life in the person of Monsignor Leo J. Battista, also of the Worcester Diocese. Monsignor Battista is a marvelous teacher, an inspired teacher, and it was my good fortune to be among the priests in our diocese who studied with him.

For nine stimulating months Monsignor Battista conducted a course in social psychology. This course, which helped me to broaden my understanding of human nature and human interactions, also included actual training and casework. The casework led me to an involvement with the Worcester Youth Detention Center, where I spent my days off ministering to the religious needs of young people. And since I'd had the training, I also performed psychological evaluations for local juvenile courts.

While ministering at the Youth Center, I came into closer contact with the Most Reverend Timothy J. Harrington, Auxiliary Bishop of our diocese. By this chance circumstance, I got to know Bishop Harrington, the third of the three men who have greatly influenced my life since my arrival in the Worcester Diocese, the other two being Bishop Flanagan and Monsignor Battista.

It was yet another priest, however, who drew me into the specific situation from which my Healing Ministry would eventually be launched. From the very beginning of my service in Worcester, I was repeatedly importuned by Father Ken Smith, the Diocesan Director of the Hispanic community, to join him in his work. His reasoning was direct. I knew the Spanish language; though not of Spanish descent, I was at least a fellow Mediterranean; and I was a man of compassionate nature.

Father Smith's reasoning made sense. His idea that I should serve the Spanish-speaking congregation was a natural. He kept after me, but for one reason or another, I didn't join him until 1972, four years after I arrived in the diocese.

To prepare for my new assignment, I was sent to Puerto Rico for a few months. I studied at the Universidad Catolica de Ponce and did field work in Los Campos. Upon my return to Massachusetts, I took up my duties in the Spanish-speaking congregation of St. Bernard's parish in Fitchburg.

This humble congregation would soon become the launching pad for the ministry God had always planned for me.

The majority of the adults were Puerto Rican-born, and they faced the same problems faced by other new immigrants —learning the language and culture and finding work. In view of their very real needs, I responded out of that part of me which I would call my "social worker" self. This response was not new to me. In fact, it was directly out of my Scalabrini missionary past. Four years had passed, and here I was, back in my previous role.

One of my first steps was to contact all the businessmen I knew in a search for jobs. I also referred people to official agencies. Most of them found work sooner or later, but some had to accept welfare. On some occasions, I collected donations from more affluent people and distributed the money to families who had to pay the rent or buy food.

Much of my attention was focused on the material needs of my congregation, but their spiritual needs were not neglected. I tried various methods to draw people into the Church and into a deeper involvement with their God. We established a Music Ministry, which gave outdoor concerts in clement weather. I recruited a large corps of altar boys.

We also experimented with serving mass in private homes with small groups of people, and we held many fiestas.

All these attempts were made with the aim of drawing people into the spiritual life of their church, but the results were disappointing. After three years, I began to wonder if I was doing the right thing. I prayed to God for guidance. It came in the form of a simple but dazzling insight.

It was Christmas morning, December 25, 1975. As I marched in procession with my altar boys and the lay leaders of the congregation, I looked around the church and my spirits fell. The pews were less than a quarter full and looked very sparse. On numerous occasions, bingo, a concert, or other social events had almost filled the church. Now, for worship on Christmas morning, the church was almost empty.

All the ways I had tried to draw my congregation to Christ had failed. The material goods and services had not done it, nor had my prayers. As I proceeded up the center aisle on my way to the altar, I looked up at the tabernacle and prayed, "O Jesus, Master, I don't know what else to try. What else can I do to bring them to a spiritual renewal, to bring them to You?"

The answer immediately filled my waiting heart: "Ralph, why not try simple, pure Me?"

The answer was like a lightning bolt through a dark cloud! The truth was illuminated. All the humanistic means I had employed to draw more people to Christ passed through my mind, a list of natural methods I'd used to bring people to the supernatural. Now God's words filled my heart. Why not go straight to Christ? That was it. My answer was there.

At that moment, God awakened my priestly heart to the powerful potential of a new ministry of Christ Alone.

When the service ended, I did not follow the custom of greeting the parishioners at the church door. Instead, I quickly returned to my study in the rectory, fell to my knees, and prayed for insight.

I was awed by the words with which God had answered my question—"Why not try simple, pure Me?" But I was not certain what course of action to follow. Could a true spiritual revival be sustained by my congregation? Could such a renewal affect people outside the Hispanic community, some of whom were prejudiced against the Hispanics and tried to ignore them with polite disdain? I wondered if all these people could be renewed into Christ thinking, Christ planning, Christ living. I wished that the answer was yes and that the renewal could grow beyond the parish, the diocese, the country. I wished it could grow until it touched and affected each and every one of God's children in every corner of the world.

My turn toward a purer, more spiritual version of Christ—Christ Alone—was not unique. Though I was unaware of it at the time, fellow priests everywhere were descrying similar situations. Our churches were emptying, and something beyond the miracle of bingo was needed to fill them again. Something beyond social activities like bazaars and suppers was needed, but that something was still lacking.

There appeared to be a paradox between sacerdotal mission and ministry. One wondered if, in the eyes of the public, the gifts of Christ were being surpassed by the tools of the world.

When I called out to God from the depth of my sincere need, He heard my prayer. He was ready to fill my brokenness with Himself, but He would not be the Christ about Whom I'd studied in seminaries. He was the Christ Who, in His Own Divine Providence, fills and directs us with His Holy Spirit.

✤

Kathryn Kuhlman possessed one of the most exceptional and true Healing Gifts of our time. She became quite well known, but I knew virtually nothing about her when she died on Friday, February 20, 1976. On that very day, however, God began to move one of the final pieces of my puzzle into place, the piece from which my Healing Gift would grow. His agents were several young members of my Hispanic congregation who approached me that Friday and asked, "Please, Father Ralph, will you let us go Charismatic?"

Charismatic? I thought. I knew that the Charismatic Renewal was a contemporary restoration of the spiritual atmosphere of the early church. I also knew the Renewal was dedicated to reaffirming the presence of the Holy Spirit in everyday life. But I had no strong personal feelings about the Renewal because I simply didn't know enough about it.

After I thought about it a minute or two, I said, "Going Chrismatic is not a fly-by-night emotional adventure. It calls for a commitment. We can only go into it if you feel that you can handle it and be faithful to it."

As soon as they left, I ran up to my room and phoned Auxiliary Bishop Harrington. I respect all powers that exist in the world unless a power proves itself to be evil or harmful. But in view of my arduous traditional priestly education, the idea of going Charismatic was a little shocking, and by then I had already been a priest for almost nineteen years.

I did not, however, reject the idea out of hand. It has always been my belief, a belief shared by many other priests, that our personal preferences must always give way and yield to the needs of the people. If the Charismatic Renewal was a road to travel toward God, I knew that I could not spurn it.

When Bishop Harrington answered the phone, I told him what had happened. "Bishop, they've asked me to go Charismatic. I'm not sure it's my cup of tea." He laughed, perhaps as if he'd expected this turn of events, and invited me to attend the Charismatic Renewal prayer meetings held in St. John's Church in Worcester.

Four days later, on Tuesday, February 24, when I went to my first Charismatic Renewal service, I was relieved because the service didn't look fanatic to me, or farfetched in any way. And I was immediately impressed by the Charismatic Renewal for two substantial reasons.

The first was the way the service completely surrounded the Eucharistic Celebration. For a Roman Catholic priest and for his people, the Eucharist is the very heart and soul of God's presence among His people. From the Eucharistic presence, people derive their strength, vitality, and nourishment.

The second essential element that profoundly disposed me to the Charistmatic Renewal was its obvious and direct connection to the most basic values of Christianity. Indeed, the Charismatic Renewal is our clearest link to the first days of Christianity, and through this link I could see that it was an enduring phenomenon.

Any further proof I needed was provided when I witnessed the inner healing session of the service.

Suddenly I saw the unity of all the segmented studies that

I'd made in the supposedly separate disciplines of philosophy, ethics, psychology, sociology, theology.

At that moment, my entire life of priestly studies fused into the eternal truth that mind, body, and spirit are parts of the whole, and I realized beyond doubt that I could best bring people to their God and God to His people through a holistic approach.

The result of my experience of the Charismatic Renewal service was to see that the Renewal was good for God's people. With this observation as my basis for action, I agreed to set sail on a new voyage of ministerial discovery.

I returned to my young parishioners and told them the answer to their question was yes. We would go Charismatic.

✻

My first contact with the Charismatic Renewal occurred in February, but the signs of what was coming, the foreshadowings of what was about to happen to me, began two months earlier, around Christmas time. My body was constantly aflame. When I touched anything, sparks came out of me. Electricity jumped out of my body. I didn't know what was happening. For a while I couldn't touch anything. At first I thought it was a static electric charge from the carpets, but it wasn't because it happened whether there were carpets or not, and it was stronger than any static charge I had ever felt before. After the electricity started, my knuckles began to hurt, and I thought I was getting arthritis. Then pains began to pass through other parts of my body, and I was frightened because I still didn't know what was happening to me. Now I can see that the Lord, in His Divine Providence, was allowing me to experience the pains of the physical body so I could respond to the pains of others. He was preparing me for my Healing Ministry.

At the beginning of May, I went home to see my mother in Providence. She was very sick, but I didn't seem to be able to help her, and I suffered in my own heart. I sat at the table in my mother's kitchen, and a rage at my powerlessness to help her came over me. I banged my fist on that table, and

I said things I had never said before in my life. I said, "Here I am, a Catholic priest, a priest! A minister of God! I am obedient to my bishop, I am submissive to everybody, I am working for the poorest of the poor; and here my own mother is suffering, and I can't even help her! Damn it!" I shouted, and I banged the table again.

That kind of behavior was completely out of character for me. I do not use that kind of language, and I don't bang furniture. The moment I realized what I had said and done, I asked my mother to forgive me, and she did.

But a little while later, when I was getting ready to leave for the trip back to Fitchburg, my mother asked, "Son, will you do me a favor before you leave?"

"Sure, Ma," I answered.

And she said, "Will you pray over me?"

"Pray over you! What?" I shouted. Her request made me angry again. "What good is it?" Of all things for a dedicated priest like myself to say, that was about the worst. My dedication to my priesthood was battling with my frustration at not being able to help my own mother. But I cooled down quickly and said okay.

My mother knelt down, and I laid hands on her head. When she got up, I left. I got in my car and drove back to Fitchburg. When I got there, I phoned my mother. She told me that after I left, she had had a dizzy spell for an hour. And she had felt something go through her body, and she had been healed of her illness. From that moment on, the Spirit was working through me. I still didn't understand or even see what was happening. But I didn't have long to wait.

Less than three months after my first visit to a Charismatic service, my own Healing Gift broke out. As part of my learning about the Charismatic Renewal Movement, I had begun attending the Charismatic services led by Father McDonough in Boston. I was at one of his services on a Saturday in early May when I felt something happening to me, and I pulled back from it and said to myself, "Oh, my God, is this happening to me?"

Some people in the church asked me to pray over them, and I felt myself, my body, filled with a new power, and the power flowed out of me and into them. "Could it be?" I asked myself, and I was frightened. I pulled back from it. I didn't even finish the prayer. I pulled away from the people. I shook my head and muttered, "This can't be." I said to my friend, who had driven me to Boston, "Let's go home." But I didn't tell him what had happened.

The next day, back in Fitchburg, I conducted my regular Sunday service which, at that time, was still a more traditional kind of service. When it was over, a few of my parishioners came up and asked if we could go to Father McDonough's again. I said, "Oh, let's not go. I don't think we should go today." I was uncomfortable at what had happened the day before.

But my parishioners were insistent, and they wouldn't take no for an answer. "Let's go, Father Ralph! Come on, we've just got to go today! And it's special too, because it's Mother's Day!" I was still apprehensive, but I finally agreed because it seemed so important to them.

We got into various cars and drove the fifty miles to Boston. They were right about it being Mother's Day. And it was also Kathryn Kuhlman's birthday, May 9. What happened to me later made it a day that I shall never forget.

When we arrived at the church, I didn't even go behind the Sacristy to speak to Father McDonough. I went to the very rear of the church, all by myself, hoping that Father McDonough would not even see me. And as I stood there, a small girl of six or seven came around with papers for petitions. She recognized me from previous services when Father McDonough had introduced me and I had preached. "Hi, Father Ralph," she said, "here's a piece of paper. Why don't you write a petition to God? Whatever you'd like."

"And what should I write?" I asked her.

"Oh," she smiled, "what is in your heart."

I looked down at her smiling face and saw that a little child was leading me. I smiled back and said all right. I took a piece of paper and wrote a message to God, a personal petition that would be placed on the altar during the Charismatic service.

I wrote my petition in three languages: Latin, Italian, and Spanish. I hoped that if Father McDonough did read those petitions, he wouldn't understand mine. Though I wrote the petition three different times in three different languages, I had no control over what I wrote. My beseechings just poured right out of me: "God, if it be Your Will, give me the fulfillment of my life as a priest. Grant me a new, complete, and worldwide ministry in the Charismatic Renewal, specifically in the Healing Ministry, the thing I have always wanted. Grant me a ministry to heal the bodies and souls of mankind."

The smiling little girl took my petition and placed it on the altar. As soon as she put it down, it seemed, Father McDonough spotted me in the shadows at the back of the church and immediately called me up to preach. I still hung back, even though I had just written that petition asking God to grant me a new ministry, but I couldn't refuse Father McDonough. I walked up to the front of the church, and since it was Mother's Day, I preached a sermon on the Blessed Mother.

The congregation was excited by my sermon, and people began clapping. They seemed to want me to say something more, maybe even do something. But I was still holding back, so I tried to slip off quietly behind the altar and be by myself. Suddenly a woman ran into the small room where I was and shouted, "Father, hurry up! Quick! My husband is bleeding inside his stomach!"

"Bleeding?" I asked. "Then you have to get him to a doctor. Let's call an ambulance right away and get him to a hospital."

"No! No!" she insisted. "*Pray* over him!"

"Pray over him? Come on," I said, "call the doctor."

But this woman would not back down. In fact, she grew even more insistent. "Father!" she demanded. "Pray!"

So I gave in to it. All right, I said to myself, I'll pray. And I did, and poom! The man went down. Just like that. In a minute he looked up at me and said, "I feel great! The pain has gone! My ulcers don't seem to be bleeding anymore!"

My natural instinct was to wonder if the man was pulling my leg. It didn't make any sense. He is bleeding, I pray over him, and all of a sudden the bleeding stops and he's okay? I felt certain he was tricking me for some reason of his own. How slow I was to believe what was happening to me.

Then I wondered if the man was crazy. He didn't look crazy, though. He was just an ordinary-looking, well-dressed, middle-aged man, and while I was wondering about him, he got up, brushed himself off, and went back to his seat singing, "Hallelujah!"

At that moment a nun came up to me, Father McDonough's sister, and she said, "Father, there's a woman going crazy here; she wants to kill her son and daughter. Will you do a deliverance over her?"

Deliverance? I thought, but the nun quickly brought the woman into the hallway where I was. I laid hands on her for about ten minutes. The woman got totally freed! She went back happy! I said to myself, "Holy mackerel! Is this real? Is this happening to me?"

My head was still spinning with wonder when a schoolteacher came out, a young girl about twenty-five or twenty-six from Cambridge, and she said, "Father, I have some problems, serious problems. Will you pray with me?"

"All right," I said, "let's sit down." So I sat with the girl in the stairwell, holding her hand. If some old-fashioned priest had walked by, he'd probably have complained to Rome. I held her hand and prayed with her, and she was overpowered. A moment later she told me, "I felt the heat go through my body, a healing through my brain."

When she went back to her seat happy and smiling, I was

left alone near the stairs in the hallway. I was in somewhat of a daze. I couldn't understand what was happening to me.

As soon as the service was over, I rushed up the side aisle of the church, trying to flee. But Father McDonough called me back from the pulpit and asked me to pray over a little crippled boy. I could not say no in front of all those people, so I went up to the little boy and placed my hands on him, and he started *moving*, and people saw this! My fear rose in one last pull, and I drew back from what was happening, but a lady cried out to me, "Father, pray over me! Touch me!" And when I did, poom! she went right down. "Father! Touch me!" the people shouted. And when I did, poom! poom! One after the other, they went down. By the time I got to the other end of the church, the whole place was laid out! People on all sides of me had been "slain in the spirit." Then I knew I had broken out. I understood that God had granted me my Healing Ministry.

Later, when I was alone in my room, I had time to think over the miraculous events of the day. I had wanted to be fulfilled as a human being and as a priest, and I had wanted my natural gift of doctoring to emerge for the good of the people. My joy is serving the people. When I wrote my petition, over which I had no control, I wrote to God from my subconscious heart. God, I was saying, I am going to give you what has been in my heart. Would you do this in my priesthood, grant me a Healing Ministry? And He did.

All my life God has been preparing me for the whole healing, the Holistic Healing. He was preparing me for the healing of the *wholeness* of man and for the healing of the *whole* world.

He must have been waiting all those years so He could say to me, "Now you are ready. You have been broken, and you have been nothing. Now you have turned to Me; you have given Me yourself with what I gave you in your life. Now you are ready for My Ministry, and I am going to lead you higher and higher and higher."

When I thought about all these things, I suddenly saw them in a new light. God had opened my eyes. And suddenly I could see the pattern of my life. The Lord had been preparing me all along for the moment when He would decide to use me as a clear channel through which He would send His Healing Grace to His people. I felt very humble and very grateful to God. "Why me, God?" I asked. "I'm not worthy of this." Yes, I had asked for the gift, the Gift of Himself Alone, but like most people, I really didn't think He was going to give it. It was truly in my heart, but I never expected to receive it. I was overwhelmed. And I still am.

Ten

DON'T BOTHER TO TOUCH ME; YOU MUST REACH OUT AND TOUCH GOD

I do not say that I can *explain* what happens during my services, but there is no doubt that these things happen. Anybody who attends can see for himself. In fact, other people can observe external things that I miss, for during a Charismatic service, I am completely out of character. It is not I. Something is in me. It is not I as a person. There is a Spirit of God functioning through me. Many people have seen this. But believe me, it is not I. Sometimes I do attempt to explain these dynamics to my congregation at the start of a service:

"During the past few years, I've noticed that many people, in their desperate need, fall into the error of confusing the channel with the Source, the gift with the Giver. They witness amazing things, and they assume I have performed them, so they reach out to touch me.

"Please don't try to touch me; it's not necessary at all. When you touch me, you're not touching anything. You must touch God alone—not me!

"I understand that you do see God in me. There is definitely no question about this. I'm trying earnestly to have God touch your lives as He uses me as His clear channel."

At other times, as the need arises, I may attempt to clarify another aspect of the dynamic of Healing:

"As I walk among you, some of you will feel electricity going through you right out of my body. Heat. A jolt of lightning, so to speak. I don't know how God does it. Curvatures of the spine will begin straightening out. Bent legs will begin to straighten. We will probably see shortened legs begin to grow. These are the ailments which seem to be healed in every service. Other ailments—cancer, blindness, or paralysis, for example—seem to be healed in clusters."

Another phenomenon which continuously and constantly occurs during our services is the "slaying in the spirit," otherwise known as the "falling under the power." This phenomenon frequently confuses the observer, especially the neophyte in the current renewal of the Holy Spirit.

To prepare newcomers at a service, I usually offer some words of explanation. I often try to use humor to relax them:

"Some of you will be falling down, or entering a state of divine spiritual ecstasy. I wouldn't want you newcomers to think we are passing out Blue Nun or chianti on the side. And there is no ether in the holy water, either. What is happening when someone falls or enters a standing ecstasy is a phenomenon of God's presence called the 'slaying in the spirit,' or the overpowering of the spirit. The resting in the Lord. The Lord usually likes to pass through people; it's a 'spirit of prayer.' The saints used to experience this type of prayer; it's called 'ecstatic union.' They were just lost in God. Their bodies, with their external senses, became suspended, and they would just float in the Lord. You have no control. So if I come up to someone and you see him fall, don't get upset.

"I will call some of you, or come to you myself. If you call me to come to you, the Lord might bring me to you, but generally I don't know who I'm going to go to. The Lord will just tell me to go up to a person, and I just hold up my hand, maybe touch his forehead, and he is healed. So let the Spirit lead me where It will because I myself don't know where He is going to lead me; this is one facet of the phenomenon known as the 'word of knowledge.'

"There is no set pattern for what will happen here today. Under the influence of what is known as 'the anointing,' there is no prescribed form or ritual required. God's clear channel must be in total surrender to the Will of God—it is God speaking, walking, healing.

"It has often been recorded in photographs, and perceived by myself and others, that during our Healing Services, my own soul appears to have surrendered itself to another Spirit, a Spirit functioning through me which causes me to be totally out of my own natural character. You will see this yourselves. It will clearly demonstrate the absolute difference between myself, the man beneath the gift, and God, the Giver of the gift. Remember, I am not the Healer.

"Another thing you're probably going to see is how I receive signals from the Lord. I will receive pictures in my mind or pains in my body which signify a healing for someone. That's the way the Lord works with me. Each of us is different. I might have the 'word of knowledge' of Healing. Then I can actually pinpoint exactly what you're wearing and the exact sickness.

"This process, by which God activates His Divine Will of Healing, differs from one Charismatic to another. It appears that the nature of each individual gift is unique. In my particular case, for example, God's Will is made known to the people in need of healing through the pains I feel in my own body.

"But please note—this process by which God works through me should not be imitated by other persons. Such an attempt would be futile, for one person cannot simply copy a gift that is distinctive to another person. Also, such superficial copying would probably be harmful to the persons in need of healing and detrimental to healing the Broken Body of Christ. There is absolutely no doubt about it; charisms are powerful forces originating from the Creator of all energy, and they are not to be trifled with."

During my years in the Healing Ministry, I've noticed that some people attend our services out of curiosity, tantalizing themselves with the unanswerable questions, "How does he do it? What's happening here?"

In addition to the curious, a surprisingly large number of whom become genuinely involved in our services, we are also visited by TV and radio journalists and reporters who wish to report on our activities.

Another group attends our services for motives which combine curiosity and professional reasons. This interesting group is composed of medical doctors, psychiatrists, nurses, and other members of the health professions. These medical people, of course, have been trained in the natural sciences. Often they come to our services for the first time with a cynical attitude. As I have heard later from some of them, when the service begins and they see things happen which natural science cannot explain, their first reaction is to assume there is some kind of trick involved. Some think to themselves, "I've got to find out what the trick is."

Of course, there is no trick. And many medical people learn and accept this as they observe and participate in more of our services, or when they examine their own patients who have received Healings from God.

In one way or another, there are frequent contacts between our Healing Ministry and members of the health professions. As a result, our ministry has been blessed by the deeply committed participation of many health professionals. Their active involvement enriches the ministry and helps to bring about the healing of the whole man, the whole woman, the whole child. This is extremely important, for Holistic Healing, the healing of body, mind, and spirit, must be the goal of all valid Healing Ministries.

Since the question of our relationship to the medical community and to the entire health-care profession is raised so frequently, it would be well to offer some explanations. In the first place, Divine Healing is not a substitute for doctors. God has made the medical man, so to reject medicine is to reject the goodness of God. As I once told an audience of several hundred doctors, nurses, and other health professionals at a lecture sponsored by the American Cancer Society and the Worcester District Medical Society, "You are God's hands, God's heart, and God's compassion."

There is no rivalry between Healing Ministries and the health professions, nor should there be. A doctor acts to facilitate the natural healing powers of the body. The medical profession is following God's laws, even if some members of it repudiate Him.

Doctors are dedicated to healing. I call on them to pray and use medicine at the same time for the healing of the whole person. After all is said and done, how great a service has been done for the man whose leg has been healed if his mind or spirit is still broken and out of touch with God?

As for how the healings actually occur, the sole answer to this question is that the Holy Spirit is at work. It is the Father creating anew; it is the Christ redeeming and delivering; it is the Holy Spirit renewing and sanctifying through the Blessed Trinity's Eternal Love.

Since God's Love and Mercy is a mystery, how can one such as I explain it? How can I or any other mortal get to the bottom of the mysteries of the Divine Romance, mysteries which by their very definition are unfathomable? The only sensible response is to surrender to God's call.

However, man's finite mind always tries to come to grips with the infinite, even though complete answers can never be gained. When one tries to find a philosophical answer for Divine Healings or attempts to analyze them scientifically, one only becomes more perplexed because there is no natural explanation available.

Divine Healing, as the name itself implies, is a supernatural power from God. However, prudence and proper discernment require us to distinguish between supernatural power from God and supernatural power from other sources. Some healings are the work of Satan, who produces superficial or partial healings as a way to entice the unwary.

If one perceives physical healings unaccompanied by inner or spiritual healings, then one would be right to question the healer. Is he really transmitting a supernatural power in the name of Jesus Christ, or is the phenomenon based on the power of Satan? And if not from Satan, is the power behind the healing derived from cosmic or psychic energies?

These questions are of great importance, for not all healings are genuine. The only genuine healing gift is the gift of Divine Healing, of which God is the Author.

God is the Author of Love and Mercy and Divine Healing. That's the only answer. God *loves* His people. "You are My people," God said, "and I have a Heart for you."

From His Heart, God brings forth Divine Healing. As He has said Himself, in Exodus 15:26, "If you will carefully listen to the voice of the Lord, your God, do what is right before Him, give ear to His Commands and observe all His Injunctions, then I will put on you none of the diseases I put on Egypt; for I am the Lord, your Healer."

The main purpose for any remarks I make at the beginning of a service is to relax the people and help them to be as receptive to God as they possibly can. I ask them to feel free and open to whatever Divine Power manifests:

"What we must do is to let the Lord simply work out this Love and Mercy in each of us. At this moment, I don't know either what's going to happen tonight. And I won't know until I fall under the anointing. There's nothing I can do about this, no way to foretell what will take place, and no way to prepare for it.

"Our only preparation for these services, in fact, is by prayer and by some fasting. All we have to be is open and receptive. God's Divine Providence is already here for us, with His Mercy and with His Love. All He wants us to do is dispose ourselves to receive His Grace. One way we do this is by prayer."

The purpose of prayer is to prepare ourselves to accept God's Will. God's Will is filled with Love and Mercy. This may not be the way we have been used to thinking of prayer, but it is a useful way.

God wants us to want Him. He wants us to accept Him. He wants us to accept Him and bear witness to His Presence, His Love, His Mercy. He wants us to bear witness to His Divine Healings.

Most of our services are intense, sometimes unbelievably so. Often I begin to feel the Word of Knowledge before I complete my introductory remarks. The unpredictable manner and timing in which the Word of Knowledge comes to me is another example of the spontaneous nature of the healing services. I never know when the Word will come, but when it does, I immediately announce or "call it" publicly.

Usually the earliest indication of a specific healing comes to me by way of an empathetic pain—where I feel a pain in my own body is the area in which someone is receiving a Healing. During a service, I might sound something like this:

"I'm feeling a pain. A healing is taking place in someone's knees at this moment. Someone who has had much physical pain. In a few moments that person—you know who you are—should jump up and say, 'Me! It's me! I'm healed!'

"A blocked ear passage is opening, or is about to. And someone who has been deaf as the result of a severe infection, that problem too is beginning to clear up. And someone wearing a neck brace is also being cured at this moment. Praise Ye, Jesus!

"The proper response to your healing is like picking up something you ordered—you must claim it! Claim your healing! Don't be afraid to identify yourselves! Let God know you are not embarrassed by His Grace! Don't forget, God loves you!"

Yes, God loves us all, saints and sinners, for we are truly all God's children.

The saint is the one who is the saint of the moment, who becomes the saint of the next. And the sinner of the moment may also become the saint of the next. All you have to do is say, "God, I made a mistake, I'm weak. I didn't mean it. I love you. Through my fault, through my fault, through my most grievous fault. I love you God." And in this way you turn right back to God.

Jesus loves us all, whoever we may be. And I've got news.

Jesus was no Methodist! Jesus was no Baptist! Jesus was no Roman Catholic! Jesus was an unmarried Jew, a carpenter's son, son of a Virgin Mother. He was the Anointed One sent by God the Father.

Jesus was Jesus, and all mankind His brothers and sisters.

Jesus revealed the Father; the Holy Spirit continues to reveal the Christ.

Jesus is Lord and Savior of the world.

As the Christ, Jesus is at the center of all Christianity. As One with God the Father, He is the Unifying Principle. Christian Unity rests on the relationship between us and God, a relationship that is the same as that between a trusting child and a loving father. When you have that relationship in which the child says, "I love my father. He loves me. I believe and trust in my father," then you have the beginning of a common unity.

There are two parties in the father-child relationship, the father and the child. And it is up to the father to be loving and trustworthy. But some fathers go about things the wrong way, like the father who set out to teach his son something about business. He told his little boy to climb up into a tree. When he did, the father said, "I want you to jump into my arms; I'm going to catch you."

"You sure, Daddy?" the little boy asked.

"You bet!" the father answered.

So the little boy jumped, but his father stepped aside, and the boy hit the ground. This angered the wife, and she said to her husband, "I thought you were going to teach him something about business?"

"I am," her husband answered. "The first thing I'm teaching him is not to trust even his own father."

Obviously this is not the right way.

Another little boy was asked to bring his father his lunch. This father was at work digging a cellar hole. When the boy got there, he looked over the edge of the hole, but he couldn't see anything in the darkness. So he called down, "Daddy? Dada?"

And from down below the father answered, "Here I am!"

"I can't see you, Daddy."

"Don't worry! You just jump down, and I'll catch you."

"But Daddy, I can't see you. It's too dark down there!"

"You jump, daddy is here."

So the little boy jumped. And his daddy caught him. He trusted his father. He believed in his father. And he was safely caught in his father's arms. Believe me, when we jump, God the Father catches us in His arms too!

We can only have unity and renewal when we recognize that God is the Father and that we are children who say, "Daddy, I love you so much, I believe in You." That is the foundation. That is a dogma; it is a belief, a truth, a confirmation, a conviction. When one believes in his father, one says, "I don't want to do anything against my father's laws or commandments. I don't want to be rejected from my father's house." So one's morality becomes an expression not of enslavement, but of love and commitment. Following this comes liturgical expression, the true, sincere inner Spirit of prayer.

Prayer, in turn, increases our openness to God, makes us more disposed to receive His Grace, and so we are brought full circle in the unending drama of God's Love for all His children.

And it is God's Love, above all, that is being expressed in Divine Healing; God's Love that is transmitted through the channel of my broken body in the form of His Healing Grace; God's Love that infuses and gives life to the whole Charismatic Renewal.

Eleven

CALL TO
THE RENEWAL

The Charismatic Renewal Movement in the Catholic Church has been growing by leaps and bounds in the past few years, and it has received much attention in the different media. But despite all that has been said and written about our Movement, a certain amount of confusion still exists. Since as yet some people are not clear about us, I will try to explain our beliefs and our purpose. Of course, this is my personal testimony, my own view of what the Charismatic Renewal is all about.

The Charismatic Renewal is in no way an attempt to create a church within a church. On the contrary, the Charismatic Renewal is part and parcel of the Church itself. As Father Martin Tierney so aptly put it, "The Charismatic Renewal is born to disappear. It is a mighty river flowing into the sea which is the Church. When it reaches the sea and becomes completely mingled with it, it will lose its identity as a separate movement and the whole Church will be renewed."

The Charismatic Renewal is less a "movement" than it is a temporary focal point of spiritual energy and love. For this reason, many people who participate in the Renewal (both clergy and lay people alike) use the word "movement" only with great reluctance. We do not seek to create factions by attaching names and labels to one group or another. We do seek unity; our aim is to bring all God's people together in the communion of His Love.

The Charismatic Renewal means living again the Pentecostal experience; it means reviving in today's church the fiery atmosphere of the Church's origins.

The Charismatic Renewal also means recreating the spiritual atmosphere of the early church community, for whom the Holy Spirit was not just a theological abstraction, but was the source of life, energy, guidance, courage, enthusiasm.

The Renewal implies restoring the true image of the Church, which is a Charismatic image, and restoring her unmistakable features, which are the Gifts of the Holy Spirit lived in the Christian life.

The root meaning of the ancient Greek word *charisma* has to do with the concept of *gifts*; not the specific thing given, but the *gift* itself. In our Roman Catholic doctrine, the *charism* is a gift of God and from God, and healing is one of its contents. The Charism or Gift is both *of* and *from* God because it never ceases to be God. That is, it never ceases to be God's power that is traveling through the mortal charismatic like myself. I am only an instrument chosen by God; I am merely a channel through which His power flows, and nothing more. In fact, Catholic doctrine specifies that charismatics like me are not even necessarily holy people. And it also specifies that the Gift is not for the glorification of the individual, but for the good of others, for the whole community.

God wants to heal us through His Church, and thus He heals us through Charisms. The Charisms have always been here, part of His Body, which is the Church. They were part of the original ministry of Christ.

Everyone has a gift: the Pope, the bishops, lay people, everyone. But there are also special gifts which God gives by nature. God wants to bless us with the Holy Spirit and raise up our natural gifts to a Charism which will help the Body of Christ. The gifts are not for ourselves, they are for the Body of Christ, for the Church, and, in fact, for all God's people.

God wants to lead us back to Himself, and the Charisms

are one of His ways. But is it not unfortunate in our own day that many of us (myself included, during the early years of my priesthood) have been forced by material circumstances to occupy ourselves with bingo, bazaars, and other secular pursuits?

It is sad to see what Catholic and other churches are forced to do in order to pay the bills. Some congregations charter buses and arrange gambling trips to Las Vegas. I think this is diabolical! It means that somebody needs deliverance!

Many people feel that they are forced into these activities, but they have got to start discerning and doing what God wants them to do. They do not have to lead others into gambling, or sell them suppers in order to pay the bills. Our own ministry has proven that. Wherever we hold them, our Charismatic Renewal services draw huge crowds. These worshipers make donations to the parish, so the parish can pay the bills. And we don't sell anything—all we do is lead the people back to God.

The various renewals of the Holy Spirit, including the Cursillo, the Marriage Encounter, and the Charismatic Renewal, share as their distinctive focus the return to Christ.

Perhaps one reason why clergymen have to turn to bingo and similar pastimes is that something is missing from much of Christian life. Psychologically and sociologically, activities like bingo are just indications that something has been lacking in the Christian spirit.

One might think that all ministers and priests would be happy to drop bingo and be free to turn to *real* ministry and be more accepting of Charisms, but this is not the case. Not yet.

That which is taking place in the Church today—the renewed presence of the Holy Spirit with Its sanctifying vitality of renewal—is bringing about the realization that all men and women are the children of one Father: *Abba*. As Kathryn Kuhlman proclaimed in one of her healing services, this spirit of renewal will be identified not in one church solely, nor in one parish, but in every church throughout the world.

As the Holy Spirit is the Soul of the Church, as it became the unifying principle of life on that first Pentecost Sunday, so this same spirit, this Soul of the Church, will overcome all disunities and unify God's people.

Some have had difficulty accepting what is happening. The actual manifestation of God's Grace is shocking to them, but this response is completely understandable. I too received a traditional, "conventional" priestly training, and I couldn't accept the healings in the beginning, either.

When I finally did accept, it was only after much prayer and introspection. I had to ascertain the source of the Healings and the form they took. Was the healing power from God? Were the healings only physical, or emotional and spiritual as well?

It soon became clear to me that the charismatic renewal in general, and the Healing Ministry in particular, were leading people to God. Since the Devil would never put Christ or God into men's hearts, I concluded the power was definitely from God.

The Devil, however, can imitate some of the healing manifestations, as can psychics, which brings us to the concept of discernment. Everyone must study and *see* what is going on in my ministry. Those who are concerned about the direction my ministry is taking should seek the answers to these questions. Are these services leading the people to Father DiOrio as an end in and of himself, or is he merely a stepping-stone to Jesus Christ and to God the Father and to the Holy Spirit? Do the people receive only physical healings, or do they receive the most important inner healing as well?

The answer to the first question is readily evident. God is Lord and Master of the world. That's *all* there is to it. He alone is alpha and omega, beginning and end.

The answer to the second question is also a positive one, but it is not as clear-cut. Some people attend our services solely in the hope of receiving a physical healing. Sometimes they receive it, sometimes not.

This extremely narrow approach to the powers of the Healing Ministry is demonstrated occasionally on my radio program. We have open phone lines, and listeners are able to call in. Most callers, almost all, in fact, seem interested in and committed to their whole being—body, mind, and spirit. But a few are shortsighted, just interested in their own aches and pains. They don't care about the bigger issues. All they focus on is the pain in their stomach or the stiffness in their leg. They feel that they couldn't make contact with me in church, and they couldn't get hold of me when they called the office; so they call me during the radio program in the hope that I'll talk to them and they'll receive a physical healing on the air. But the Apostolate of Healing is not that simple. We do not want people to get the idea that all they have to do is dial Ralph for a healing.

I am not a computer programmed for healing. I am, simply and in truth, a conduit chosen by God to transmit His Love and Forgiveness to all His children.

But those who misunderstood the Healing Ministry, or tried to use it for quick relief of their physical aches and pains, cheated themselves. Also, their shortsighted, self-centered approach to the Healing Ministry raised questions in the minds of my superiors. As is their duty, they exercised prudence, examined my ministry, and soon gave it their blessings when they observed that the direct and ultimate object of the healings was the salvation of souls.

In my ministry, the Holistic concept of healing for the total man or woman is basic. If God, in His Divine Wisdom, uses the peripheral manifestations of the body—a phenomenon like the "slaying in the spirit," or prophecy—these occurrences are just stepping-stones toward the inner healing of souls and the healing of our relationship with God. The miracle of Healing resides in the fulfillment of man's relationship to God and is the very salvation of the soul.

In Catholic philosophy and theology, we have a phrase

which explains the physical manifestations of healings, instant or progressive. The phrase is *invisibilia per visibilia,* to the invisible by way of the visible. The invisible things of God can only be seen by us when they are manifested in something visible. God's Grace and Love, for example, are invisible. They exist in the spiritual realm. To bring Himself to us, God has to come in *visible* signs.

In the Catholic Church, and in the Episcopal Church as well, we have the Sacraments. We say God's life comes to us through the Sacraments. The life of the Catholic Church is the Sacramental Life and the Sacraments are made visible to us through external signs or symbols.

Water, for example, a tangible element, is taken aside, blessed, and it becomes a Sacrament by which we can conduct or transmit the gift of baptism.

At the Last Supper, Our Lord took the bread and wine, also made of natural substances, and He blessed them. He changed the bread and wine into His Body and His Blood, which come to us in the gift of the Eucharist. So in the form of visible artifacts, Sacraments are instituted, and God brings His Invisible Life to us through them.

The repeated concept of God making His Invisible World visible to our human understanding brings us back for another look at the manifestations which take place in the Healing Ministry. This time we must consider them in the context of today's world.

The world has become atheistic in many ways. Occultism is on the rise too. Some people are following false cults which are based on black magic and many other diabolical ideas. These false cults are contrary to God's first commandment: I am the Lord thy God. You shall have no strange gods before Me. That is the great commandment which everyone must uphold. God is angry with man's betrayal. As a contemporary evangelist has said, "Anything that keeps us from God's best is sin." There is sin and betrayal. More than ever, the world is in need of holistic healing.

To serve the need of His people, God is doing what He

did in earlier times. He is expressing Himself through signs and wonders to bring His people back to Him.

Though some continue to be amazed at God's behavior and hesitate to accept the manifestations as being valid, it has all happened before. As my own Bishop Flanagan once stated during a television broadcast:

"The Healing Ministry is a phenomenon that has become very much emphasized in the Charismatic Renewal during these past few years. But actually it goes way back in the tradition of the Church, way back to the New Testament, where Jesus healed. When He sent His disciples forth, He told them, 'Go forth and cure the sick and say that the Kingdom of God is at hand.' So I think we must realize the fact that the Healing Ministry still has a function and a role in the Church today. . . . In other words, Jesus Himself made it very clear that the whole purpose of His ministry and His mission and His cures was to bring people to Him, and so I feel that it's important that we not over-emphasize the physical healing, but rather the total healing of the men and women—the physical, emotional, and the spiritual."

With the manifestations of His Healing Grace, God seems to be saying, "I'll show you My Love! I'll overpower you with the abundance of My Being. You will be drawn to accept Me and be healed."

In His omnipotence, God causes healings which go far beyond simple medical cures. He causes instantaneous healings. He propels a paralyzed man from his wheelchair. He rekindles the light in a blind girl's eyes.

He causes people to sit up and take notice. He shakes them out of their complacency. He startles them into confusion, a healthy confusion which leads to knowledge. First they ask, "Are my eyes deceiving me? Is what I am seeing actually real? Are these things happening?"

And out of their newly aroused uncertainty, doubting Thomases are led to reconsider the Mystery and the Love of God.

So the physical manifestations are one of God's visible ways of speaking to His people, and as such, the physical manifestations should not be scorned. They must be understood.

✦

The role filled by a Charismatic like myself is all-encompassing and amazingly intense. God is on one side, filling me with His tremendous energy, and mankind is on the other side, seeking the energy as it passes through me.

God, of course, uses me as He wills. All I can do is try to dispose myself to Him and His Grace. Human beings, however, present a different situation. As people often do, they behave emotionally or become confused. In their wonderment, some people confuse the puppet with the Puppet Master.

No matter how frequently I implore, even admonish people, some of them, much to my chagrin, approach me as if I was the source. They attempt to touch me.

As I often repeat at the services, people do not have to touch *me*. When they touch me, they are touching nothing, or, at most, another human being like themselves. They must reach out and touch God.

And they must reach out and touch each other, a phenomenon of communal sharing. They must reach out and touch each other, must demonstrate their love and concern for each other, for this is one of the highest expressions of our love of God. It has been a great source of satisfaction that one result of the Healing Ministry has been the development of strong communal and spiritual solidarity among the people who attend the services.

During Healing Services, one can sense and actually feel the abundant supportive prayers which well-wishers offer up on behalf of those in need of healing. Such unselfish expressions of brotherly and sisterly love must warm God's Heart.

Twelve

~~~~~~

HOW I EXPERIENCE
A HEALING SERVICE

Many people ask me to explain what is happening during a healing service. I cannot truly explain it because I simply don't know how God does it.

During a service, I enter a state of being that is neither consciousness nor unconsciousness, but a mixture of the two. In this trancelike state, I am aware and unaware at the same time.

In the early days of my healing ministry, I was confused by what was happening to me. But as time passed and my experience grew, I understood that I myself am "slain in the spirit" during a service, that I enter into an ecstatic union with God and so am completely under His power. Some authorities have called this state "under the anointing."

I make no pretense at being able to describe *how* God works, but I can describe how it feels to me. . . . During a service, I am out of character. It is not I. Something or Someone is in me. There is a Spirit of God that is in me, working through me for the good of His people.

I can only describe how the Lord seems to be producing these effects through me personally. Maybe with other charismatics, He does it in a different way. With me, it starts with the sensation of tremendous heat. Sometimes it's like a volcano. Sometimes it comes out of me like the heat from a microwave oven. First I feel it in my hands, then in my whole body.

There are also external phenomena during a service which seem to be out of the ordinary. People often say that I seem to be aflame. I can't be or appear ordinary because God is overpowering me.

Then I have the Word of Knowledge. I feel a pain in my eyes or a pain in my ear. A pain in my knee. And at that very moment, when I feel a specific pain, the pain forces me to call it. "There's someone being healed in the knee," I will say. "Please identify yourself." And usually the person will stand up. Or I will say, "Someone is being healed in the back," and I will point to the exact spot in my own back where I am feeling this pain. This is the spot in which some person is being healed.

Sometimes I describe exactly what I am feeling. With ears, for example, there are different sensations. Sometimes my ears pop open, and I will announce, "Someone's hearing has just popped; someone who has a hearing problem, your ears are popping open now or will pop soon." Other times, my ears throb and seem to open slowly, a little at a time, and if this happens, I will call it. "Someone's hearing is beginning to open; your ears are starting to unblock."

The physical knowledge I receive through the medium of my own body is from God. His Healing Grace is being sent to one of His people through the clear channel of my body. I feel it in my body as if I myself suffered from the disease or infirmity being healed. The pains I feel are not as acute as the pains suffered by the person being healed, but sometimes they are very strong.

Some healings make themselves felt before a service begins, but usually the pains begin after the service has started. The pains linger until the person identifies himself or herself and claims the healing. Some people are too embarrassed to claim their healing in public, so the pain lingers within me after the service is over. And some healings take place after the service is over and the person is on the way home, or already there. It is truly a mysterious process, and neither I nor anyone else knows how God does it.

Several members of my ministry, those people who are

very close to me, including my own mother who is a healer herself, also receive the pains. If one of my ministry receives a pain which I don't, he or she will tell me to call it, and I will, and usually a healing is claimed.

It is the way the Lord makes the invisible known to the visible.

In the beginning of my healing ministry, I received knowledge only through the pains in my body, but soon I began to receive pictures in my mind. It doesn't matter if my eyes are open or closed, if I'm facing the people or have my back to them. I often see the area of the body that is receiving the healing, and I may see the clothing covering the area. Sometimes I see all the clothing. Sometimes a piece of jewelry, such as a necklace or a bracelet.

Sometimes before a service I feel completely drained of all energy, but once I'm in the sanctuary, I am galvanized. There is a power, an energy, that enters my body. I don't understand it, but I recognize it and am cognizant of it. At times I say to myself, "Where is this power coming from? I'm filled with life!"

Then, near the last five minutes before the service ends, my eyes sink in, my strength drains away, and I feel I'm going to collapse. By eleven-thirty on a Thursday night, I am ready to drop. I can hardly walk. The evening service starts at seven, but by then I have already held a morning service which may have run five or more hours. If I am walking among the people at the end of the service, I get so thoroughly exhausted that sometimes I don't think I can walk back up the aisle.

But up to the moment when exhaustion overcomes me in the closing minutes, I am alive with an incredible energy, filled with a strength that is not mine. It is God, living in me and using me.

During a service, power of knowledge comes into me of what God wants to transmit in this moment from His eternal Mind, through the spoken word, through scripture reading, and through association with the people in the pews. I may look at a person and come right to that person without knowing what I'm going to say. Then I receive a Word of Knowledge, and I tell that person what's wrong with him—what's in his heart, what he is suffering from. At that moment, I feel that I have a body that is now severed from DiOrio. But there is another power in me, and I can penetrate right through a person.

A girl who was healed of diabetic blindness was told by her friends before the service to look into my eyes. I understand what was said—it is no longer I looking at that girl. It is another power, and it is not the I of Ralph DiOrio.

Often I will feel an energy go through me, an energy of knowledge, which causes me to say to a particular woman, "You have arthritis, and you are going to be healed!" I say this with not even a shade of doubt in my mind. I'll call this person, and I'll turn to a pew filled with people and say to one individual, "Come here to me; you have colitis," or I'll feel compassion for another particular person.

If I fail in the spirit of compassion, if I become a little negative toward someone, it usually indicates to me that God is not intending to heal the person at that time. But if I have full compassion, actually feel the core of a person's being, all of God's strength that's in me goes out of me and into that person. Then the healing takes place.

My feelings of compassion are also from God, God working in me and telling me that this or that person has something in him or her that needs to be cleansed before the real healing takes place, and sometimes I will find that there is a bitterness in such a person, or hatred, or lack of forgiveness of a sin that first has to be surrendered. It is God working through me completely. It's no longer the human me.

Sometimes I feel the Word of God come right into me and force itself out of my mouth, out of my soul, to express itself.

At times it happens that my humanity might struggle for the words to express what's taking place, and all of a sudden the words come out. I proclaim a healing of blindness, and I quickly say to myself, "Oh, my God, what am I saying— am I crazy?" But God made it come out, and this is what happened with the blind girl who was told to look into my eyes.

During that particular service, I called out healings as God led me, but something made me tell the people: "I know God is working through me, and sometimes my humanity steps in to try to hinder what God is doing. I myself, within my human limitations, am always afraid to say certain difficult things, but today I'm going to step up my faith and let God say what I'm saying. I feel that there is a healing of blindness taking place—God is bringing a healing to someone with eye problems." Two or three ladies popped up with eye disturbances, their eyes were burning and they said they could see better. For the time being, I let the matter sit there.

At the end of the service, I passed through the body of the church, praying with people while holding their hands. At that moment, some members of my ministry brought a blind woman to me near the altar and said, "Father, this woman was blind and now she can see."

Several days after the young woman's sight was restored, she appeared on our radio program and gave the following testimony. I think its beauty speaks for itself.

"My name is Patricia Pannet, and I'm twenty-two years old. Four years ago I lost my sight due to diabetic retinoscopy. It happened so quickly that I was totally blind in a matter of three weeks. I had been under a doctor's care for about three years, and I had had some eye surgery to help regain my sight, but a few month ago I had lost the function of both of my kidneys, and I had come up to St. John's to pray for my father who was going to give me a kidney to save me.

"The surgery was scheduled, and I had come up because I had wanted to ask God to please free my mind from the burden of thinking that something would happen to my father under surgery because I love him very much. He was making a very big sacrifice for me, and I thought nothing about my eyes at that point as I was more intent on my father. As I was sitting there, I was concentrating very hard on my father and praying for him and experiencing all the healings, but at that point I could not see anything in the church.

"Right then, the people I was with wanted to leave the church, and I, as a matter of fact, said, 'No, thank you, I would rather be healed.' And as I sat there I looked up and noticed that I saw some lights, and I looked down again as I often see flashes, and I thought, well, maybe I'm just getting caught up in the experience and I don't want to have this be a false thing. So I sat there for a couple of minutes and I noticed that my eyes started to burn, and again I pushed it off because my eyes often are filled with pain. But I looked up again and saw the lights, and I noticed that they were all in a row. They started to become clearer to me and I saw more lights. As they became clearer I noticed that they were windows, and I saw the shapes of the windows and the panes and the color of the opaque glass, and light was coming through the windows and it showed outlines of people's heads and faces that I had never seen before.

"In the time that I had lost my sight I had had periods where my sight was good enough to see some shadows, but now I saw colors and objects, and I stood up on the kneeler because I wanted to be sure I was seeing what I was seeing. I looked around the church and I saw faces and styles of hair and colors of clothes and the sizes and shapes of people's bodies, and I turned around and I looked behind me and I noticed that there was a choir there, and there was trim and I could tell where the trim ended and a different type and shape and color started. And I looked over further and I noticed a round disc, and as I stared at the disc I noticed it was a clock and I walked out to the aisle with the ushers and I was looking at the disc, and as I was looking at it my sight was becoming clearer. And I thought it really was a dream and that I would just wake up and find it had never happened, but as I looked at the clock it got to be very clear to me and someone asked me what time it was and I said about three-thirty and that's approximately what time it was.

"Then someone dragged me up to the altar. I was stunned. I couldn't move. I was just so taken aback by the whole thing because I was seeing so many colors and shapes and objects that were very close to me, and my sight was improving as seconds were passing and I was very afraid because I thought it was a dream, and I said, 'No, I'm going to let Jesus into my heart and let Him do His job because I'm trying very hard.' And so I went up to the altar and I met Father DiOrio, and I told him what had happened and I told him why I was there. I told him I was there to pray for my dad, and he prayed with me. The Holy Spirit entered my body, and at that moment I felt so free and so relaxed from all the tension I had been going through for months, deciding upon a transplant and how I was going to save my life without hurting people. I had been going through a lot of pain and anxiety for a long time in dealing with my life, and now that it was affecting my family, it was even worse.

"Father DiOrio prayed with me, and the Holy Spirit entered me, and I felt that what I was doing was the right thing and no matter what happened, as long as I had Jesus' Love with me, He would walk beside me in whatever I did, and I felt very free, as if I could float away, and I passed out. I woke up and I was very, very warm and I was sweating, as a matter of fact, and I was looking at Father DiOrio and I noticed what he was wearing and I noticed his face, and his features became very clear to me. Features which I could not have distinguished in the preceding four years. I noticed his eyes because someone had told me to stare at his eyes. They said that I would be able to see heaven if I stared through his eyes. I couldn't see them very well, but as I looked and looked at his face I saw his eyes, and I noticed that they were blinking, and this was a new experience for me because I really didn't remember what it was like to have somebody's eyes blinking at me. And then I noticed that he didn't have much hair and I told him that. I felt very stupid because I had forgotten that there were a million people in the church. I turned around and I saw people and colors, and everything just became very clear to me. I sat in a chair and I was looking around the church, and things became clearer. That was last Thursday, and ever since then my sight has been improving. I can't say my sight is like a normal person's, but it has improved, I would say, about ten times.

"It's a joy for me to pick up a cup and know where the handle is or to look at the clock and know what time it is. Or to look out my front door and see that there's somebody there and not be afraid of shadows that I can't truly see. Or to see my mother's face.

"Ever since that day in St. John's church, my sight has been improving and I just thank Jesus for that, and I think He's with me and I think everyone should be with Him and open their hearts to Him."

In His Healing of Patricia's blindness, the Lord acted swiftly and with little foreknowledge to me. When I'd called her Healing, the words seemed to fly out of my mouth of their own accord.

�֍

During a service, God acts through me in various ways. Sometimes I feel electricity leave my body. People have described their feeling of being hit by an electrical current when I touch them, or even when I hold my hand a few inches away. Sometimes I might touch a person just with my fingertip, and sparks actually fly—I and others have heard them crackle. They go right out of my index and middle fingers. Once when I held my fingers close to a woman's abdomen, electricity sparked right out; it could be seen and heard, and the woman was thrown over to the ground.

Another time, in Fitchburg, I called out a healing, and a woman said she felt as if a bolt of electricity hit her; she was knocked to the ground, and her back, which had been bent, straightened right out.

These manifestations of heat and electricity are not unique to me. Others who are in the Healing Ministry also experience these things, so it's the same spirit.

The electricity, or force from God that seems to us to be like electricity, can work at a distance and even over the phone, as numerous experiences during my phone-in radio ministry have demonstrated. Healing and "slayings in the spirit" over the phone seem remarkable, unbelievable, but for God, all things are possible.

Leroy Jenkins, another healer, says he knows there's going to be a healing when he gets goose bumps on his legs.

To me, it happens perceptually. I might see a picture. I might see the Holy Spirit just floating around and landing on a certain object—a person's breast or a person's eye. I might see everything in the church in blackness, and in the blackness I might see a small Holy Dove float down and land on a person's lips or eyes or ears, and I see light and I call the healing of the places on which the Dove landed—the eyes, for example, or the neck or the stomach.

Or the Holy Spirit touches someone on the mouth and I call the healing of a mouth disease, or I see a person in blue or pink and I'll call it. I'll step out on faith because I know God is working through me. By now I have gone through so much that I'm absolutely convinced that God is working through me.

There is no telling how God will choose to work through me. Once, in a morning service, I was at the front of the church facing the people, my eyes closed in contemplation. I saw a dark universe, and suddenly I saw a box kite floating across the darkness. The bands of paper around the kite frame were bright green, and the kite floated at an angle, slightly tipped. I watched the green box kite floating in the darkness, and instantaneously the Lord made me say, "There's a woman . . ." Why did I say woman? "There is a woman here who is suffering from a phobia of flying and of height. As a little girl she fell off a ladder, and this is why she is afraid of heights. And this is affecting the healing of an ailment she has in her body."

A woman in a bright green dress came up from her pew and said she was booked to fly to Florida, and she was very frightened. She was afraid of flying and of heights. And she had fallen off a ladder when she was young. She also had arthritis and a stomach ailment.

I prayed with her, and she was immediately "slain in the spirit." She went down as if a bolt of lightning had knocked her to the ground. When she woke up, she didn't know what had hit her. It was one of those "slayings in the spirit" that are very powerful, and she said, "Father, I'm not afraid anymore." When I asked how her arthritis felt, she smiled and said the pain was gone. She was totally healed.

In this instance, God used an image of a box kite that had to be interpreted to grasp its symbolic meaning.

Her fear took a bodily form, as arthritis. She was delivered from the spirit of fear, and when she woke up, there was no longer a physical problem of arthritis.

God, at that moment, wanted to heal that woman who had a psychological block which had produced a physical ailment. But in order to heal her arthritis, which was only the symptom, her deeper psychological problem had to be healed, for it was the cause of her physical symptom.

✤

My eyes can be closed or open when I see the Holy Spirit. I see it as a light or as a Holy Dove. Sometimes I see this during prayer. At other times, when I first get a glimpse of something, I find myself closing my eyes. One day at the front of the church I had my eyes closed, and I saw all the pews receding in an exaggerated perspective to the rear of the church.

The pews were all black, cones of blackness going away from me, and the aisles were all light—solid white light— cones of solid white light with the wide ends closest to me, as if light were pouring in from the aisles.

I saw this image as a battle between light and darkness, and I said there was a woman who was torn between coming to God and running away from him, and these clashing forces in her life had driven her to the verge of suicide. "If you will identify yourself, God will give you the fullest of healings."

A woman came right up the aisle, crying, and she told me she wanted to kill herself. "It is my struggle that you just described." I prayed with her and blessed her, and she had a deliverance.

This happens frequently. Jesus is in control, not I. He's teaching me. One day, I called an ailment. I said there was a woman wearing white and some type of violet or beige. She had abdominal problems, an ulcerated colon, to be specific. "Will you identify yourself?" I didn't let up—I kept calling it. Finally a woman cried out, "I've got something on, it's beige!" I called her to come forward, but the color was not beige, not the beige I had seen in my mind's eye. Now, I could have saved face, but I said, "You're going to get a healing too, but there's a woman here with something beige—come forward!" And at that call, another woman did come up. God was saying to me, so to speak: "Of course, you could have saved face, but it wouldn't have been Me." This woman was wearing the color beige I had seen. God told me to call *this* one!

One day I called, "There is a woman here in blue with cancer. A woman in blue on the right side of the church is being healed of cancer."

All of a sudden, everyone started screaming, "Father, here she is!" A woman in blue, on the left side of the church, said, "I have cancer, Father; please help me, help me!" I said, "God is going to heal you too," and for the moment, I stopped talking. I thought to myself, Well, there she is. You better take her; she's on the left side, not the right side as you said, but I thought, God, if this is really You and not me, it's got to be the right side. Otherwise, I'm false.

So I said, "This woman will get her blessing and be healed, but the one I called is on the other side," pointing to the pews on the right. "You are in blue. Come forward! You have cancer! Where are you?" And finally, after all that, a woman in blue stood up and came forth. The whole congregation screamed. This woman was "slain in the spirit," and she received a healing. I kept calling her, stepping out on faith because she was the one God wanted to be called.

This has happened to me many times. The lesson I have learned is that I must always follow the Word of Knowledge from God and not act on my own human thoughts.

There are a variety of ways God acts through me. Sometimes God's words just bubble right out of me, with no thought by me at all. Other times, I must interpret symbols, like the green box kite or the cones of blackness and the cones of light. The Holy Dove, a Holy Light, or different visions I have are yet other devices God uses in His Healing Ministry.

Thirteen

~~~~~~

DIVINE HEALING AND THE MEDICAL PROFESSION

There is much misunderstanding about the healing ministry. We must consider that in this world there are wounds that await everyone on the road to perfection. We all need God's constant healing action. We must seek to avoid misuse of the gifts by handling them with prudence. Prudent people, though they are sensitive to the feelings of others and may make honest mistakes, will nevertheless take necessary safeguards. The gift of healing is a manifestation of the Spirit whereby a physical, psychological, or spiritual healing, or a deliverance from spirits of oppression and possession, or a renewal occurs. These manifestations are primarily a result of God's action.

It must be remembered well at all times that Divine Healing is not a substitute for medical care. The healing ministry is not against the medical profession, against doctors, against the use of medicine just because the power of prayer and God's power to heal is invoked. On the contrary, the doctor's professional skills, his medical knowledge and insights, are invaluable. These are God-given treasures. To reject medicine is to reject and deny the goodness of God.

Divine Healing is not simply a case of mind over matter. Jesus accepted the reality of physical suffering, and Jesus did something about it—He healed. There is no record of His having ever said, "Your problems are just in your head." Instead, we are told again and again that He was filled with compassion and He healed. Jesus knew suffering Himself, and because of this, He understands us, loves us, and heals us.

Spiritual Healing or Divine Healing is not just positive thinking. Certainly, a positive attitude on the part of the sick person and those about him can be important in healing. We are dealing with the whole man. It can sometimes make the difference between living and dying. However, positive thinking does not save, and the Healing Ministry is involved with the salvation of the whole person. Spiritual Healing includes a person's relationship to Jesus Christ. Furthermore, Spiritual Healing is not just relief from pain. We must guard against using the Lord as a hot-water bottle, taking Him off the shelf when we hurt and putting Him back when the pain is gone.

Spiritual Healing is not faith healing. Often we hear the lament from a sick person: "I am not getting well because I don't have enough faith; I just know it." How tragic. To make healing dependent on the quantity of faith is to turn faith into a good work. Yet seriously ill people often crucify themselves, blaming their lack of healing on the smallness of their faith. All we need is a faith the size of a grain of mustard seed which, as Jesus said, is the smallest of all seeds.

Yes, I know personally that coping with a serious illness can so consume a person's resources that there is no strength left for trying to build faith. But it is not the moment of my faith that heals; it is my *faith* in Christ that He *can* heal. Jesus said to the woman healed of a hemorrhage: "Daughter, thy faith has saved thee; go in peace." (Luke 8:43–48.)

It was her faith, her faith not in herself, but her faith that Jesus *could* heal her that mattered. How true. The faith healer tarnishes the work of the healing ministry. People put their faith in the so-called healer, be it man or woman, rather than in Christ, and by this route some people undoubtedly experience a physical and even a mental healing, but they are not healed in spirit. They are not made whole in a faith relationship to the Christ.

Spiritual Healing is not spiritualism. Many tend to confuse the two. Spiritualism supposedly heals with the aid of departed human spirits, whereas Divine Healing calls only upon the third person of the Trinity, the Holy Spirit.

Thank God for His creations by which man is able to mature and grow. I know many physicians, surgeons, nurses, dentists, laboratory technicians, and a variety of therapists in both the physical and mental areas of the health professions. I value and respect their education, their research, and their experience. I, along with other divine healers, accept the skills of such men and women who have dedicated their lives to easing and eliminating the sicknesses which beset mankind. And yet all of us firmly believe that all healing is of God.

The physician may set the stage for such healing; yet he cannot command the bruised flesh, the torn tissue, the shattered bone to restore itself to perfection. There are times when the medical specialists must confess that they have reached their limits. But God is not bound by such limits, and sometimes God applies the balm of Gilead when man despairs of the cure.

Divine Healing often seems to violate logical sequential thinking based on the natural laws of cause and effect. But Divine Healing is not caused by prayer cloths, water from the Jordan River, or financial bargains made with God or with His healers. The cures, the deliverances have come because of man's simple faith. In the healing ministry of the Holy Spirit, God is demonstrating His power over Satan.

The ministry of Divine Healing does not urge a person to disregard his medicine, to cancel his doctor's appointment, to request discharge from the hospital. If I pray for safety as I travel, God does not in turn ask me to cut the brake cables on my car to prove that I have a valid faith in Him. Moreover, Divine Healing brings forth a simple statement of faith—the simple call for a simple faith in a God who cares for every little sparrow that falls! A God who cares for me. It is a call to couple God's healing ministry as manifested by medicine with his healing ministry made manifest through His Holy Spirit. It is not a call for one to refute the other.

In many cases, there is no apparent scientific reason why a person is healed. In some situations, the case seems hopeless, not treatable in the sight of man. Fortunately, the word hopeless is not found in God's dictionary. Yet I am quite aware, as are others blessed with the divine ministry of healing, that many illnesses are psychosomatic in nature, that the will to live, faith in the creative work of the healer, temporary remissions of certain afflictions, or a faulty preliminary diagnosis are factors that need be considered where divine healing is claimed. But if we are not careful, in the process of explaining away divine healing, we may explain away God and our salvation.

I am convinced that at times God allows us to go beyond our faith in physician and penicillin. His infinite wisdom bridges the gap, the healing streams flow down, and the Great Physician performs a work of physical grace in the life of one of His children. This miracle of physical healing is no greater than the miracle of spiritual healing which every Christian must acknowledge as truth and reality for his or her own life. There are times, however, when God appears not to heal, at least not physically. I doubt Jesus healed everyone He met while upon this earth. In fact, it is substantiated in the Scriptures that Jesus could perform no miracle in His own town because His own townspeople would not accept Him. Therefore, He had to leave His town and go to those which would accept Him.

Why does God not heal in all cases? To this large, perplexing question I do not have the answer. Perhaps it is because He is a God who sees the total pattern that is being woven in all of life, while I see only what seems to be the misplaced thread.

No magic formula emerges to assure a Divine Healing. I did not find that God healed only after so many hours of prayer or so many days of fasting. God does not seem to demand an anointing-with-oil ceremony or a laying on of hands by spirit-filled men or women, although often the two practices are involved in the healings.

God seems to tailor his preconditions to each case at hand. Even in cases where the sick remained sick, where the dying died, I personally, in the four years of my formal healing ministry, have recognized healings. Paradoxical as it sounds, when a pain-wracked physical body has succumbed to the ravages of a disease which God did not choose to heal, there was complete and glorious victory over the affliction. It was a type of healing to which every Christian can testify, for we know that when this corruptible body of ours puts on incorruptness, when this mortal corpus puts on immortality, we will experience healing in the most permanent eternal sense of the word. This is the Great Healing, the Healing Unto God.

Of course, no one likes to see another person die because of the separation in our hearts and souls, but when you've become Charismatic and if you've really got love and faith, then you *know* that death is just a stepping-stone to Eternity. Then you're not afraid to die, especially if you're doing the best that you can and you know that God has affirmed you.

So the Great Healing, of course, is to Death. There comes a moment when these physical and natural healings of the earth will stop, and God will just give us the Big Healing unto Eternity.

❖

One's belief or disbelief in Divine Healing pivots on one's answer to several questions: Is the Bible true? Is Jesus Christ true? Was Jesus actually a miracle worker? Was He the Son of God? Is Jesus' promise in John 14:12, which testifies that His followers shall perform even greater works than those which He did, still pertinent for us today?

How shortsighted they are who judge us in our Divine Ministry of Healing, for they are really judging God's promise to us. Each person must answer those questions personally in his or her own conscience, thus determining how great his or her God shall be. For me personally and for people like Oral Roberts, Father McDonough, Vickie

Jamieson, Leroy Jenkins, and all of us who have been called authentically to the Divine Ministry of Healing, the questions are all answered by a clear-cut *yes*. I believe that God answers prayer. I believe that God heals.

Fourteen

SOME HEALED,
OTHERS NOT—WHY?

It is always a pleasure to pray for the sick. But one of the greatest pains that comes to us who have been blessed with the Healing Ministry is the question: Why are not *all* healed? Any valid healing ministry has to face this baffling question. And we do not always *see* the manifestations and the signs and the wonders on every occasion. Why is this so? The answer very simply is, "I do not know."

When I pray for someone and no healing seems to take place, I have compassion for that person. My own human awareness is not always active during a service. But when I am present and aware of what is happening, my heart leaps up at healings and breaks apart when no healing seems to come, especially when I pray over a child with no apparent result.

As always, in a moment of anguish and pain, when confronted by a person in desperate need of healing, all that I can and must do is step out of the situation and let the Christ step in.

I understand that the healings are from God, and I know enough to realize that I will never completely understand how or why God works. Nevertheless, when I pray over a person and no healing seems to come—no apparent mending of a broken body, no apparent lifting of suffering and pain— my own heart bleeds with compassion.

There is no easy answer to the problem of suffering. It will always remain a mystery centered in the Cross. Once, I remember, I laid hands on a woman who had cancer, and she received an immediate healing; this was confirmed by her doctor. (We have the case in our files.) But a year later, this woman became sick with another ailment, an infection accompanied by a fever. Again I prayed with her, but the infection took its full course, and she apparently received only the blessing of the spirit. Why was there physical healing in the first instance and not in the second? The answer remains, "I do not know."

Cases such as this one are puzzling, but we must face the fact that such experiences occur in the Healing Ministry. It is impossible to explain these things. All that we can do is to place ourselves as fully as possible in our Lord's Hands.

There are so many factors which could inhibit healing. The sick person may not be ready for ministry, either emotionally or as regards faith in God. If this is so, the Holy Spirit does not lead us to pray for healing.

Some people still believe that God sends suffering either to purify or to punish. How wrong this is. How often people say, "It's my cross," or, "I am a wicked man, I deserve this," and many of us priests and ministers were wrong when we taught that "it's your cross, bear it." No, God does not give us burdens. He asks us to help Him carry the Cross of Humanity so there should be a purpose to our pain and suffering.

Another major reason for the lack of healing is that large numbers of Christians still do not believe that Christ will heal. Or even if they're not Christians, they do not believe that Elohim is really a God of love and mercy and a God of healing.

This brings us to another question—*who* can be healed? The answer is, *anyone and everyone!*

The people who attend our services represent all humankind. They come from all backgrounds, all nationalities, all denominations. They are the rich and the poor, the black and the white, the young and the old, the believers and the doubters. All God's children, and all God's children are not Christian.

I believe the gifts of healing are available outside the

Christian religion. I see healing as an expression of God's Love for His children, and that means everyone, Christian and non-Christian alike. For example, we have had Jews attending our services, and they too have received healings.

Jews may not accept Jesus Christ as their Messiah, but they believe in Yahweh, God the Father. In the Old Testament, in Exodus 15, God said, *Ani Adonai Rofeeka. I Am The Lord That Healeth.* God spoke to them. He was coming to heal them. His whole ministry, His whole relationship to mankind after the fall of Adam and Eve, has been Healing.

Despite the wonders performed in Biblical times and the healings taking place today in Healing Services around the world, some people have not surrendered their doubts.

Large numbers of Christians believe that Christ can heal, but have not sufficient faith to believe that He *will* heal. Such a burden of doubt must affect our ability to receive the healing love of Jesus. And for this reason, it is very important that clergy instruct their congregations and their priests, ministers, and those working in pastoral counseling and hospitals to find joy in the vocation of dealing with the sick and the broken in body. Pain can become a channel to inner spiritual life, to healing, to a new relationship with God the Father, Jesus Christ, and the Holy Spirit.

Sometimes healing is blocked when there is unrealized or even unrepented sin, or an unwillingness to forgive. Forgiveness, the act of forgiving, is a central concept. We must forgive those who harmed us—those who did things which hurt us by acts of commission and those who hurt us by acts of omission. We must forgive those who did not love us enough.

If a child—and we are all children—feels that a father or a mother did not love him enough, even hurt him and made him feel great pain, I say to that child, "Forgive your father! Forgive your mother!"

Imagine that you are a child and that one of your parents has hurt you, has caused you terrible damage by something done or not done. And imagine that that parent comes to you and asks for forgiveness. And imagine that you say, "Yes, I forgive you!" In that moment, you are free!

As Jesus said of Lazarus, His friend whom He raised from the dead, "Unbind him, and let him go." In these words is the substance and full meaning of the act of forgiveness.

Once you release your enemy, you are free. The release is there. And that outlet of freedom is generally seen through tears, external tears which we hope are sincere, flowing from the heart. When you forgive your enemy, you are free to be healed through the Christ Who forgives.

So when praying for healing in the emotional life, in some cases one has to reach deep and go to those unexposed hurts. It may be that the person concerned cannot yet bear to recall what has been such a shattering, traumatic experience of the past, and so healing will be delayed.

Another answer to the question, "Why are not all healed?" takes us into the spiritual realm. We must always remember that the cause of trouble may be demonic, rather than physical or emotional. This is why a valid healing ministry cannot just proclaim physical or emotional healings: such results could be produced by psychic powers or even by the Devil. But a valid healing ministry eventually has to end in the Ministry of Deliverance because deliverance is completely and directly contrary to Satan who tries to destroy the soul of man.

Thus you see that the Ministry of Healing is not necessarily straightforward. Many factors are involved, and therefore, should there not be an immediate healing, we need not be discouraged. Jesus Himself told us to persevere by seeking and knocking.

In spite of these difficulties, we should continue to pray for the healing; we should continue to lay on hands, to call in those priests and ministers who are balanced Charismatics and let them lay hands on us with sincerity in what God is doing and even anoint us with oil as many times as may be necessary. And as we do these things, we should ask the

Holy Spirit to reveal the blockages that are delaying healing. Where healing is administered with an honest and a good heart, with responsibility and seriousness, God always acts to bless. Difficulties should not make us lose heart, but on the contrary, they should force us into a life closer to Christ.

We should not pretend to *understand* God's ways. The answer to the question of how the healing works remains the same. We do not know. While it does seem that a positive attitude toward God helps, such an attitude is not necessary to achieve a healing.

We must remember that we are dealing with Divine Healing, not faith healing. Faith healing would be a quantitative phenomenon based on the amount of faith brought to the situation by the person in search of a healing or by the faith healer. In Divine Healing, God is the sole author. God works through a person's physical body and into his inner life and makes a total change, for the real miracle of Healing is Spiritual Healing.

God has His own Purposes, and that is the Mystery of God. But I do know that God calls everyone to salvation, to the holistic healing of spirit, mind, and body. God uses anything and everything to bring His people back to Him. That is the purpose of healing.

Fifteen

~~~~~~

LEO PERRAS
WALKS AGAIN

An individual's attitude toward me personally or toward my ministry is not the factor which decides whether he receives a healing or not. Frequently, it seems that people who are asking for a healing for someone else are themselves the recipients of a healing. One such instance was the case of Leo Perras, who received a healing that allowed him to walk again after twenty years in a wheelchair.

Before the service began on that particular day, a member of my ministry told me he felt I was afraid of the wheelchairs. He said I wasn't paying attention to those in the wheelchairs parked in the front of the church because I was afraid that they represented too large a process of healing. Then he said he felt as if God had given him a message for me. "Don't be afraid of the wheelchairs," he told me. "Remember, God is the Healer, not you."

During the service, which was a very powerful one, I neither sought nor avoided the people in the wheelchairs. But three hours into the service, while I was facing the altar for a moment, I suddenly found myself thinking, "Lord, if this is real between You and me, let me see broken bodies straightened out, let me see people rise up out of wheelchairs and walk today." I turned around, and my eyes fell on Perras.

I had noticed him earlier in the service—one of the people in wheelchairs parked at the front of the church. I had never seen him before that day. But as soon as my eyes fell on him, I felt as if a magnet was drawing me to him. Next thing I knew I was standing beside his wheelchair, looking down at him.

He looked like a broken man, fatigued and haggard. I laid hands on his head, and with firmness and determination I said, "Rise and walk in the name of Christ!"

Perras looked up at me as if to say, "What are you, some kind of a nut?" But the Word of Knowledge in me would not be denied, and I remained firm. "Rise right up and praise God! Stand right up! Praise Ye Jesus! Praise Ye Jesus! Walk! Walk in the name of Jesus! Do not be afraid!" At that moment he took my hand, rose up out of his wheelchair, and stood. He wobbled, but he stood. "Praise you Jesus! Thank you Jesus!"

That day Leo Perras received a powerful healing. Several months later, he gave a testimony which describes his experience far better than I could:

"My problem started back in 1939. The original injury was caused when I was hit by a loading cart in the factory where I was working. Of course, before World War II they did not do direct spine operations, so they had other treatments for me, but complications set in.

"In 1950 there was another back operation, and in 1952 another one. By 1958 I started falling; I'd walk, and I'd fall. So they decided to do an exploratory operation, but something went wrong, and when I woke up I was paralyzed from the waist down. I was told then that it was mechanically impossible that I would ever walk again.

"A year later, like all paraplegics, I developed an extreme amount of pain, what they refer to as 'intractable pain.' So they decided to do a chordotomy, which is an operation in which they go into the neck area and sever part of the spinal chord to do away with the pain. Of course, there were a lot of side effects that weren't contemplated—my left arm was left in very bad condition.

"Well, the chordotomy didn't do too much for pain—I was

on Percodan in the daytime and injections of Demerol at night. So four years ago, they did an operation in which they implanted an electronic unit in my chest and an emitter at the base of my skull inside the spinal chord. I carried a cigarette-pack-sized control unit, and I could tune the emitter the way I wanted. Supposedly, this unit would blot out the pain. But it only worked for six or seven months, and then it failed. I went back to the Demerol, the Percodan, and sleeping pills too. At times the pain was unbearable. This went on until August 27, 1978, when I went to Worcester and attended one of Father DiOrio's services.

"I went to St. John's mostly to pray that a problem my daughter was having would come to a resolution. The most I hoped for for myself was to get rid of the pain, which was very bad. My condition seemed to be deteriorating all the time.

"About three and a half hours into the service, the pain was at a point where I was considering leaving. I couldn't take it anymore, and my hopes were not very high. I am a lifelong Catholic, but I had never been to a Charismatic service before, and I had never set eyes on Father DiOrio before that day.

"But just as I was about to leave the church because of my unbearable pain, Father DiOrio came up to me, blessed me, put his hand out, and said, 'Rise and walk in the name of Christ.' For the first time in twenty years, I was face to face with it. I don't know what got me up, but I got up. I still can't explain it.

"Father DiOrio told me to touch my toes, so I bent over and touched them. And then he asked me how long I'd been in a wheelchair, and I told him twenty years, and he said, 'You and I are going to go down the center aisle of this church to the front doors and back,' and he was walking backward and I was following him. I went all the way down and came back.

"It was the first time I had walked in twenty years. I

became very emotional. I laid in the sanctuary for about fifteen minutes, getting my emotions back. When I got back to my wheelchair, my wife asked, 'How do you feel?' And I said, 'I feel great!' She said, 'You do?' And I said, 'I don't have any more pain!' And since then I have been walking, and I have not had a bit of pain. Several hours later, we left St. John's Church and went back to East Hampton where I live. The first place we went was to my doctor's. I had been giving him grief, phoning him at night and everything else because of all my problems. I said to my wife, 'This is where I have to go first.' She said it was late. 'You're not going to pull him out of bed?' And I said to her, 'For this? Oh, yes.'

"By the time we got to his house, we were three carsful of people. My wife rang the bell, and at first there was no answer. She rang it again, and a voice called out, 'Who is it?' My wife said, 'It's me, Bertha Perras; would you mind opening the door?' I was standing right in the center of the doorway, waiting for him. When Dr. Mitchell Tenerowicz opened the door and saw me, he grabbed his head and said, 'Oh, my God!'

"A short time later, Dr. Tenerowicz was asked by the press to comment on my newfound ability to stand and walk. Dr. Tenerowicz said, 'Neurologically, it's impossible. He's walking on legs which are so emaciated from years in a wheelchair that, anatomically, they shouldn't support him. Even to expect this man to stand up on his legs, balance himself, and walk—I just believe this has to be something nonmedical, the work of the Holy Spirit.'

"I have been walking since that day. I have had no pain, and I have used no medication. Everything is great. I have a whole new life. Praise the Lord!

"I was told that I was a hopeless case, that I would never walk again. But what has happened to me has gone deeper than just a physical healing. My new spiritual life is far greater than what I had before. This whole experience is fantastic, and my whole outlook is different. I talk about Jesus to everybody I see. I just can't shut up about Him."

Since that day in the summer of 1978, Leo Perras has been leading an active life outside of the confines of his wheelchair.

Sixteen

A PRAYER
OF THE AIRWAVES

Oh, Father in Heaven, Lord Jesus, Oh, Holy Spirit! My heart just breaks as I think of the broken body of Christ out there, of so many people in need. To them just bring Your healing power.

Lord, we ask You through this message, this prayer of the airwaves, to bless that person with arthritis, that person with asthma, that man or woman who suffers with bladder trouble, all those who are in agony through bone fractures, the patients who suffer with cancer or leukemia, persons who have cataracts of the eyes or cirrhosis of the liver, ear trouble, Lord Jesus, emphysema, eye trouble, headaches, heart disturbances. And that man, that woman with high blood pressure, or any other infection, Jesus, just bring Your healing power. And there are those suffering with influenza, kidney ailments, pneumonia or stomach trouble, tumors of all sorts. To them, Lord Jesus, with the power of Your Holy Spirit bring Your power of healing.

And Lord Jesus, there are those special deliverances that have to be accomplished to bring health to Your people. Go right now out there to that man, to that woman who is suffering with alcohol, that other person with anxiety, and those suffering depressions of all forms. Lord, just heal them in their anger with themselves and others or with situations, and, deeper than that, let them have self-contentment and know that You love them, that they are important.

And to that person, that man, that woman, that child, that teenager who's suffering with despondency or discouragement or doubt, Lord, bring Your hope.

Heal that person who is addicted to drugs or to sex without love, rather than to love with sex and responsibility.

Lord, bring healings to families that are in trouble, to that one husband out there, to that one wife at the point of breaking. Their marriage is in trouble, Lord; just heal them.

There is so much pain in so many areas. Heal the person with sadness and emptiness and loneliness. Heal those who have sleepless nights, Lord Jesus. And heal those secret sorrows, Lord Jesus, and those tensions that bring pain.

The man or woman who's trying to surrender tobacco, give them a gift, Lord Jesus, the grace of temperance. And that person with unbelief, oh, Lord, be the object of their life, their hope, their belief, their love.

Heal us, Jesus, in our weakness and our worries. Lord Jesus, we have come before You. We ask that You bring Your healing power, the fullness of Your Holy Spirit. We ask this through the blood of Christ and in His Holy Name. Amen.

✤

This is the kind of prayer I am likely to use at the opening of a radio broadcast. I got involved with radio as a logical extension of my work.

In my Charismatic Renewal Ministry, it became clearer and clearer to me that my basic purpose was to bring the good word of God to man. This comes down to evangelism. Pope Paul VI told the Bishops of the world that we now needed evangelization again. Teaching, instructing, and renewing the people back to God. He issued a proclamation which recommended that evangelism be the program of the Church for the next few years. I was already immersed in this, so the Pope's proclamation and his appeal to the Bishops of the United States, asking them to accept his point about evangelism, served to confirm further what God had done for me in 1976.

I was considering ways to broaden the evangelical impact of my ministry when a communications specialist came to me and suggested I do a radio program. The idea pleased me immediately. I had had experience with radio back in my

Utica, New York, days when I did the *L'Ora Catolica* program, and I knew that a radio program could satisfy the countless people unable to get to my services. It would also allow me to bring my ministry to the shut-ins, perhaps the very people who needed my ministry the most.

Earlier, a Boston television station had done a story on one of my services, and a woman received a healing through her television set. The station did a story about her later on. This eposide made me see that television and radio were both acceptable media for my ministry, that they were perfectly good channels through which to spread the good news of God to the greatest number of people. These thoughts were in my mind when I received the suggestion that I use the local radio station to reach a wider congregation.

My Bishop gave me permission to try it for a few weeks, but now I have indefinite permission to carry on my radio ministry.

✤

On the radio, I have the same Word of Knowledge as I have during my regular services. People receive healings right over the telephone or over the airwaves.

We broadcast on a local Worcester, Massachusetts, station, but people hear about the program all over the country, probably from friends and relatives or from personal visits to our services. So during our broadcasts, we have had phone calls from all over the country, from as far away as Hawaii.

Phone callers just burn with the heat while I'm praying with them—on the telephone with individual callers and over the radio with the rest of my audience.

We have to ask God how these things work. I do not even pretend to understand them. But I do know that *anything* is possible for the Holy Spirit.

✤

The Apostolate of Christian Renewal implies restoring the true image of the Church, which is a Charismatic image, and restoring her unmistakable features, which are the gifts of the Holy Spirit that live in the Christian life. It is a praying

Church, a singing Church, a healing Church. The Hour of Healing aims to offer hope and blessings to the thousands of people who are coming to the realization of God's love for man.

People from all over are constantly coming and jamming places of worship. People from all walks of life, of all denominations, are uniting with healers such as myself in that one great act of man—praising God.

Thousands come. Many too are turned away from lack of space. Wonders of spirit, of soul, and of body are being witnessed as they are performed solely by the Power of God.

❖

After an opening remark such as this, it is my custom to begin each program with a prayer which serves the purpose of placing the Healing Ministry, and the healings that may take place, within the context of the complete Christian life. One of my favorite radio prayers follows:

❖

Oh, Holy Mary, our mother, the mother of God, the mother of God's children, how great you are. You have given to the world your Son, Jesus Christ, and thus you became our mother, my mother. All who would have God as their Father would have you as their mother.

So therefore, dear Mother, today and every day of my life I accept you as my queen, as the queen of heaven, as the very treasure of life, as the ever-flowing channel. You brought the very Author of life and of grace, Jesus Christ, our Lord, and by becoming the mother of God made Man, you did become likewise the mother of my redemption.

Oh, Mary, on this day and every day of my life, I renew my baptismal promise as renouncing Satan and everything that he offers, and as a sign of your pleasure, dearest Mother, just pray for my parents, be they living or deceased. Pray for our Holy Father, John Paul the Second, who is now becoming that living martyr for humanity. Pray for all the priests throughout the whole world, missionaries, ministers who serve your blessed Son with faith and hope and love and with sacrifice. Pray that we may have zealous and holy vocations and that we'll go forth to change the world and not be changed by it.

And grant that our men, be they young or old, may love you as St. Joseph loved you, that they may be found more frequently at your shrines, imploring your protection and your guidance. And let all women imitate more and more your modesty in dress and in bearing, and grant that mothers, by their love for you, just instill into the hearts of their little children a deeper devotion to you. And grant that our children will always fly to you for protection and gather around you as Jesus did.

Oh, Mother, you are our guiding light which leads to the discovery of God. Just give us the wisdom of the crib that leads to the strength of the Cross. So as a perfect model of all virtue just raise us, your children, to the height of sanctity, and as a mirror of justice just help us to see and to correct our daily faults.

Oh, Mother, we are yours in time and eternity. Amen.

❖

Since it is always the purpose of my ministry to bring about holistic healing, I always stress the fact that the physical manifestations are not ends in and of themselves. They are one of the ways God uses to bring His people back to Him and to a life of virtue. On this particular broadcast, for example, I followed the prayer to our Mother Mary with this comment:

❖

My friends in Christ, you who are our radio audience, you who are now listening to my voice, you have made this consecration with me to Mary. You now belong to Mary; she is your mother. She will give you life, the life of her Son. So go to her and she, like a gentle mother, will not only be the mother of your Christian vocation, but she'll nurture that vocation with the food of her Son, bringing you to Him.

You'll be surprised to see how Christ will be brought to you and you transformed into Him, making you another living Christ. This is a good and healthy vocation. So let Mary show you that the life of God is the life that is worth living, that life can be beautiful where God is. For where there is God, there is paradise. As St. John Mary Viannay used to say, "A soul in union with God will always be in springtime."

❖

By this point in the broadcast, all the telephone lines in the radio station are jammed with calls from people trying to reach me. They start calling long before the show even goes on the air. And the prayer lines at the St. Joseph's House of Prayer, which are manned by members of our prayer ministry, are also jammed.

When I am not available to answer the calls, the messages are taken, and later I read as many of the requests for healings as I can, usually at the start of the program. After I read them on the air, I offer another prayer:

❖

Lord Jesus Christ, we ask You to accept our nothingness and to receive the prayers that come from our spirit and our heart which are in union with You. There is no healing in any of us, Lord Jesus; You are the Healer. Send Your Holy Spirit at this very moment to all these people. Lord, just send Your healing power.

And may God the Father bless each one of these persons and may God the Son heal them and may God the Holy Spirit give them strength.

May God the Holy Undivided Trinity guard their bodies and save their souls and bring them safely to their heavenly country when time on earth ceases and eternity begins. We ask this through the Blood of Christ and we cast these sicknesses and diseases out through the Blood of Jesus and His Holy Name. So be it. Amen. Thank You, Jesus.

❖

At this point in the broadcast, I begin to take some phone calls personally. The conversations I have over the telephone with people who are seeking prayers and healings are very revealing, for they show what is on the minds and in the hearts of those who come to our services. For these reasons, I present a sampling of these telephone conversations.

FATHER DiORIO: Hello, you're on the air.

ELDERLY WOMAN: Father DiOrio?

FR.D.: Yes.

E.W.: I was healed at a Thursday morning service. Father, I'm calling for my dear friend; she has asthma so bad she can't get to the service. We used to go every week, and now she's laid up and also my brother-in-law who has a bad back. Could you please pray for both of them?

FR.D.: Yes. We'll be glad to. When did you receive your healing at St. John's?

E.W.: In August, Father.

FR.D.: What was your ailment?

E.W.: If you remember, arthritis in my hands. You picked me right out from the audience, and then you said I had something else worse, but it was my husband who had it.

FR.D.: How are you doing now?

E.W.: My doctor says I still got to go to him because of my overweight. Otherwise he would let me go.

FR.D.: Keep healthy and well. We'll pray for your intentions. Thank you.

E.W.: Thank you, Father.

FR.D.: Lord Jesus Christ, by Your patience and suffering, You hallowed earthly pain, and You gave us the example of obedience to Your Father's will. Be near right now to these people who are calling their weaknesses and their pain, Lord Jesus, and go into those hospital beds right now, Lord Jesus, with Your wounded hand, and place that wounded hand of the wounded Healer upon these wounded seekers and bring about a complete healing. We ask this through Your precious blood. Amen.

E.W.: Thank You, Jesus. Thank you, Father. I'll pray
   for you.
FR.D.: Thank you, good night.

The next call was from a woman who was so distraught
that she could hardly talk through her sobs. She was calling
about her husband who had a serious blood disease. "Pray
with me, Father," she pleaded. "Help me to help him!"

FR.D.: Beloved Father in heaven, we ask You at this
   very moment to bless the tears of this woman which
   are symbolic of the pain and suffering that's within
   her heart for someone who You gave her in the holy
   bonds of marriage. Bless her tears that she may assist
   him and care for him and save his soul as well as
   take care of his body. Lord Jesus, just strengthen her
   first; give her the sufficient Grace, Lord Jesus, just
   to be Your Grace to her husband, and, Lord, let this
   man receive the fullest of healings. We ask this
   through Christ, our Lord. Amen.

This distraught woman, talking through her sobs and
tears, said, "Oh, my God! Thank you very much, Father, I
shall always remember you. Thank you and God bless you!"

FR.D.: Hello, you're on the air.
YOUNG WOMAN: Father?
FR.D.: Father speaking.
Y.W.: I was calling with the hope that somehow I . . .
   I have a drinking problem, and I was wondering how
   best to solve this . . . even though I've had some
   medical help . . . not much, but . . . but it's with
   me, and I don't really know how to solve it . . . I
   . . . ah . . . I've been a manic depressive . . . taken
   lithium . . . and lithium causes you to tremble, and
   I found out that alcohol would cure the tremor, but
   now I've got a compound problem, where if the
   alcohol cures the tremble, the alcohol has gotten
   into my system. . . .

FR.D.: Yes, I understand the problems of alcoholism, so why don't we just pray right now, and just give you to the Lord Jesus, okay?

Y.W.: Yes, Father.

FR.D.: Father in heaven, we just ask you to bless this woman right now, Lord Jesus, and go right down to any psychological cause, from childhood or into her youth, Lord Jesus, and the age at which she is living right now. Let her realize, Lord Jesus, that there is no need to be angry with herself or with society, that she's really accepted as she is, Lord Jesus, and let her have self-contentment, the lack of which is a basic cause of so many external, painful frustrations. Now we ask You to heal her in her central nervous system and any part of her brain that could be about to be hurt right now by this toxic alcohol poisoning. We praise You, Father, we thank You. Give her a complete healing. May God, the Son, heal you and God, the Holy Spirit, give you strength, and may God, the Holy Undivided Trinity, guard you and protect you and preserve you all the days of your life. Amen. God bless you, and we'll continue to keep you in our prayers. Thank you for calling.

Y.W.: Thank you, Father.

The next call was from a woman whose husband and children had all left the Church; she wanted our help in healing and restoring their faith. It was a request that went right to the heart of the matter, for she was asking for spiritual healings for the members of her family. In her name I offered the following prayer:

FR.D.: Lord Jesus, we ask You to look at the heart of this mother. The word *mother* is a word that means suffering and pain, but there's also joy at the base of that pain, and we ask You, Lord Jesus, to heal her intentions right now for her family, that all may be as one. Jesus, You made Mary and Joseph a Holy

Family with Your presence. Reunite this family now, morally and spiritually. We praise You, Father; we glorify Your Holy Name. Amen.

After that, a call came from a woman named Mary. As is sometimes the case, people who have been to some of my services in person call to tell me what has happened to them, and this woman was one of these.

M.: Hello? Father DiOrio? My name is Mary. I went to your service three weeks ago down at St. John's. I have had a broken hip and I had surgery on my hip, and since I went to your service I have not had to use a cane. I've been walking a hundred percent better.

FR.D.: Praise the Lord!

M.: Praise the Lord, Father.

FR.D.: God really blessed you that day.

M.: Yes, He did.

FR.D.: Praise God.

M.: Yes, Father. Thank you so much. Father, I have a friend who has a problem. She had a shock, and she has great difficulty with her speech. I told her I would ask you to pray for her.

FR.D.: Yes. Lord Jesus, we ask You to receive the prayers of this woman right now who has called in with gratitude for what You did to her, and we ask You, Lord, to accept her intercessory prayer for that person close to her heart, her friend. Praise You, Jesus, and thank You. Thank you for calling, Mary.

M.: Thank you, Father DiOrio, and God bless you, dear.

When I hung up the telephone, I experienced the Will of God the same way I experience it during a service in church, and I announced it as I felt it:

"I am going to call at this moment . . . I feel the Word of Knowledge working in me . . . someone in our radio audience has received a healing. A healing has taken place as you're listening to this radio program. You have received a complete healing in the renal area, the kidney area. You had a problem with the right kidney. You're feeling the warmth of the Holy Spirit going right through you at this very moment. On your return to your doctor, you'll find that there is a total healing. As this healing is completed, we ask that you notify our office and praise God with a service of gratitude. Amen."

Once a woman phoned in with a list of illnesses and ailments a yard long. She had phoned during a previous broadcast to ask for a healing for her leg problems, but this time she was so distraught and upset that I had to calm her down. So I said with some firmness in my voice, "Just try to listen to me for a moment. Please try to forget everyone and everything and all the anxieties that you have. Let us pray together right now, with trust and confidence in the Lord Jesus Christ. Okay?"

CALLER: Yes, Father.

FR.D.: I'm going to ask you to compose yourself.

C.: Yes, Father.

FR.D.: Compose yourself with tranquillity and with trust in God. Lord, we ask You first to bring a healing to this woman's mind and relieve the stress and nervousness and anxiety she's going through. I'm going to ask you now, with trust in the Lord, to sit down in a chair right now.

C.: Yes, Father.

FR.D.: I want you to raise your legs up.

C.: Yes, I am.

FR.D.: One leg is shorter than the other.

C.: Yes, it is, Father.

FR.D.: The right one.

C.: Yes, Father.

FR.D.: I want you to close your eyes and place yourself

in the trust of the Holy Spirit. You're going to feel warmth go right through you, and that leg is just going to come right out. It's about a half to three quarters of an inch shorter, isn't it?

C.: Yes, Father.

FR.D.: Just trust in the Holy Spirit. I want you to forgive the person who has hurt you most in life. This will bring about the healing. Do you forgive the person who hurt you most in life?

C.: Yes, Father.

FR.D.: Do you really mean that?

C.: Yes, Father.

FR.D.: Surrender yourself totally to Jesus. I want you to pray with me.

C.: Yes, Father.

FR.D.: Lord Jesus Christ, I come before You, I consecrate my being to You. Out of my nothingness . . .

C.: My what?

FR.D.: Out of my nothingness I ask You to bring healing to me as You raise me anew. Praise You, Jesus. Thank You, Jesus.

C.: Thank You, Jesus.

FR.D.: Lord Jesus, send Your healing power to this woman right now. Lord, just elongate that leg, and heal with Your Holy Spirit her spinal area, Lord Jesus. Cleanse her, Father, purify her, let her take her mind off herself to recover from her despondency. Just take it right out of her, Lord Jesus. We rebuke that spirit that's been in her, Lord Jesus. Let her find peace and joy and tranquillity to give herself completely to You. Praise You, Jesus. Thank You, Jesus. Amen. So be it.
What are you feeling at this moment?

C.: Not much.

FR.D.: Look at that leg. How is that leg?

C.: It seems to be getting a little longer!

FR.D.: Stand up, please.

C.: Yes, Father.

FR.D.: Touch your toes, please.

C.: Yes?

FR.D.: Did you touch them? Can you hear me?

C.: I'm kind of deaf in one ear, Father.

FR.D.: *Touch your toes!*

C.: Touch my toes?

FR.D.: *Yes.*

C.: Okay.

FR.D.: How are you doing?

C.: I touched one toe!

FR.D.: Touch all your toes with both your hands.

C.: I touched the toes of my two feet with both my hands, Father!

FR.D.: And there's no pain?

C.: No.

FR.D.: Praise the Lord! God bless you!

C.: Thank you, Father, very much, and God bless you.

FR.D.: You're welcome, dear. Praise You, Jesus.

So once again we come to the close of our program. Christ Jesus, we thank You. We know that many people are being healed out there through Your Healing Grace. You are the Power and the Glory forever. Amen.

Seventeen

A HEALING
UNTO THE DEATH

In addition to regular services, the radio broadcasts, our telephone prayer lines, and our guest appearances in various places throughout the country, our ministry is also involved with weekend retreats. At these, other aspects of a true healing ministry are revealed.

One of the approaches that we have found valuable is a husband-and-wife team from our ministry to deal with the problems of troubled marriages. The salvation and healing of a marriage is of great importance, for not only is marriage a holy bond, but it is a union that involves at least two people and, if there are children, even more. So the healing of marriages is high on our agenda.

Perhaps one of the most moving testimonies given at one of our retreats came from a middle-aged man. In his words one sees revealed God's true Spirit, one sees God's hand touching His wounded children with His loving mercy. This man's testimony concerns a Healing unto the Death and into eternity:

"A year ago I was here with my mother to make our retreat. We left my father . . . a father of fourteen children . . . we left him very, very sick. He had cancer, he had an aneurysm next to his heart. He had come here himself and received a spiritual healing. He got us all together, and he told us that he was dying and that he was going to meet his Creator and that he wanted only one thing. He was ready to meet God; he said God was living in him. But he wanted to be with us, his family.

"When I was here that weekend a year ago, I prayed to my

God with all my soul, and I told Him in these words; I said, 'Jesus, You have given my father all the love that You possibly could. There is no more time. This has got to be it. He will not make it through the weekend. It's got to be tonight.' And I told God, 'You made that body. You have fabricated it; You are capable of putting it back together. You are not only capable, but You can if only You want to. But if this is not Your will, then I'm going to ask You one thing. Relieve him, relieve my father of all his sufferings because his wife and his fourteen children whom he raised by working hard and never taking a day off in his life for sickness, those fourteen children can no longer bear to have him suffer so.

"And it seemed as though I had my dad in my arms, and I was praying to the Lord for some Grace, and I offered him to the Lord. Perhaps Father DiOrio intervened, for the Lord took my father from me, and He gave him to Jesus. I never saw him alive again.

"My dad is in heaven today; I know that. My brothers and sisters know that too, and the fourteen of us, as our father wished, have given ourselves to Christ."

Eighteen

LEAD THOU ME ON, O LORD— THE FUTURE OF THE APOSTOLATE OF HEALING

Many people have asked me what I think is in store for me and for this Apostolate of Healing. It is an interesting question, but I do not always approach the future that way. My future is in the moment. I want to fulfill the present to the best of my ability as I stand in the presence of God.

Each moment God is unfolding my ministry as He wills. God's word will tell me the future, and since I am only human, that knowledge has to unfold moment by moment.

But let it be YOUR *unfolding, Lord; let me have no moral or spiritual block. Let me have no lack of faith, no psychological barriers. And grant me physical health, too, Lord, that I may fulfill Your ministry.*

My future is in God's hands. All I do is ask God to let me fulfill the moment according to His will. Whether He grants me life for another hour, another week, or another year, let me unfold and fulfill His plan for me and for His Apostolate of Healing. Let me bring His Healing Grace to all His children.

As it is, we see thousands—tens of thousands—of people who come from all over the world to attend our services. They arrive in chartered buses from all over the country, particularly from the New England states, New Jersey, New York, Pennsylvania, Illinois, and Ohio. Others fly in from Europe and South America specifically to attend our services. I never know who is liable to show up at one of my services. Once a tribal chief from Samoa, who happened to be in Washington, D.C., on official business, came to Worcester just to attend my service. On another occasion, a whole family came all the way from Sidney, Australia—all they did was to telephone first to make sure I'd be giving a service when they arrived.

I see these people coming to find God, be it in the first hour of their existence or in the eleventh hour of their being. Some even come seeking to use God as a Band-Aid. God will be their Band-Aid, even if it's in the last minute of the day, because in that minute might be their last chance for conversion unto God.

✤

At the beginning of my healing ministry, I was afraid to accept the fact that God had actually chosen me, Ralph DiOrio, to be one of the clear channels for the sending of His Healing Grace. I doubted at first. I asked, "Is this really happening to me, or am I dreaming?"

But after a while, so many remarkable things occurred during my services, things I saw with my own eyes, that I had to accept the reality of what God had done to me.

Around that time, I went on a retreat in New Jersey and happened to meet a fellow priest who, though himself not chosen distinctively by God, could see and discern what was happening to me. He told me that I had to face the truth, *that God had selected me distinctively*, and that I should no longer try to cover it or deny it out of the fear that others would criticize or condemn me.

This understanding priest told me I had to be honest. His counsel was wise. He gave me the strength that I needed to face the awesome truth of what had happened to me that afternoon when God's Healing Power began to flow through my body, as if a gigantic faucet had been turned on full force.

"All of us priests can pray for the people, and some healings will take place," this wise priest told me, "but what we can do does not compare to the way that God is *distinctively* using you. You have no right to be apologetic for what God is doing."

Whatever happens, I am a Roman Catholic priest with priestly duties to perform, and I must perform them according to the ways of the Church.

I am subject to authority and have no intentions to be disloyal to my diocese or the Church. I want to function within the Church, and I believe I am doing so with the proper guidance I have received through Bishop Flanagan and Bishop Harrington, and through the assistance of the many nuns and priests with whom I've come in contact. Among the staunchest of these, in his unflagging devotion to the Apostolate of Healing, is my dear friend and colleague, Father John P. Kochanowski.

I believe I am being directed by my superiors, my colleagues (nuns, ministers, priests), and by lay leaders to give glory to God. I am being guided and supported to bring salvation to souls through the healing manifestations that do occur. This I truly believe.

As 1979 and the entire momentous decade of the 1970s drew to a close, our ministry entered a new phase of its existence. In November, two years almost to the day on which I had been reassigned to St. John's parish, I left St. John's and moved the Apostolate of Healing to our new home, the St. Joseph's House of Prayer in Leicester, Massachusetts.

The reasons for our move were practical ones. In the first place, our ministry, by its very size and intensity, was beginning to intrude on some of the other activities in the parish. And in the second place, we simply needed more room.

Our new home, formerly known as the St. Joseph Convent, was renamed by us the St. Joseph's House of Prayer. It is located directly to the west of Worcester, from whence Bishop Flanagan came to bless our new home during a

ceremony and a special mass conducted before the House
of Prayer officially opened.

St. Joseph's provides us with ample space for our administrative and secretarial offices: studio space for our radio
and television apostolate; and a telephone room for our
prayer line staff.

We also have a chapel, which is open from nine in the
morning to nine-thirty at night for adoration and private
prayer. Our prayer clinic staff is available for consultations.

When I am in residence, I conduct a daily prayer hour
from 12:00 noon to 1:00 P.M. for the members of our staff
and for visitors.

Since the outbreak of my charism in 1976, our Apostolate
of Healing has grown by leaps and bounds. At the time
of this writing, over 300 active volunteers participate on a
regular basis in one or more of the ministries which have
been organized. These ministries include music; telephone
prayer lines; prayer clinics; radio and television work; intercessory prayer; transportation; publications; ushering; and
active participation in Healing Services, which includes the
task of catching and easing people to the floor as they are
"slain in the spirit." The Apostolate of Healing has wide-
ranging activities, but there are volunteers to assist in all
of them.

Our full-time regular staff, of course, is much smaller.
These are the people with whom I have daily contact. Beyond their specific duties, they provide something which no
Apostolate like ours can do without. These wonderful, God-
loving people freely and joyously offer their moral, emotional, and spiritual support for the good of the healing
ministry.

Our secretaries include Alice D'Agostino, Mary Bari-
beault, and Aline Beaudry. In addition to their office
work, these women answer the thousands of phone calls
which pour in from all over the world and at any hour
of the day and night. They also open, read, and attend

to our mail, which amounts to over a hundred pieces each day.

Our public relations director and right-hand man is Vincent Librandi.

And finally, the special assistant to the entire Apostolate of Healing is my mother, "Molly" DiOrio.

My mother is a holy woman, a Christian woman. She lives in the presence of God, and she is a woman of character. She adds a great deal of love and energy to our Apostolate and respects it greatly. But then, of course, I am her son.

Nevertheless, my mother has also seen objectively that my vocation has been anointed and confirmed by God. The blessing I've received has also been a great joy to her. She has believed in God's love for me ever since I was born. In serving our ministry, she is not merely serving her own son. She is serving and adoring God's Grace as it operates through my broken body.

Though my mother and many others were willing to believe in the validity of my charism at once, my superiors were obliged to exercise more caution. Their duty was to investigate my charism and establish whether it was valid or not. Their responsibility was to act prudently and follow established procedures.

At every step of the way, Bishop Flanagan and Auxiliary Bishop Harrington have supported me. After proper discernment, they declared my charism to be valid. Later, when the far-reaching implications of the Apostolate of Healing became more clearly apparent, Bishop Flanagan granted us permission to place the Apostolate of Healing under a board of directors.

Our board of directors is a unique organization. It was designed by my Bishops, several of my colleagues, several lay people, and myself. We created this new design in order to respond more directly to the expressed needs of God's people.

Both clergy and lay people are on our board. Among the clerics are Auxiliary Bishop Timothy Harrington, Reverend John W. Barrett, Reverend George Lange, Reverend Francis

Scollen, and especially Monsignor Leo J. Battista, director of the board, director of the Catholic Charities of Worcester, and my longtime mentor.

The lay members of our board include a psychiarist, two lawyers, and an accountant. The wide range of experiences represented by our board members affords us the resource of wise and varied counsel.

Under the design of our reorganization, my duties were more closely focused on spiritual matters and completely given over to the Apostolate of Healing, of which I am director. Also, we were given the freedom to make our own judgments about the numerous invitations we receive to conduct healing services all over the United States and in many other nations around the globe. With God's love, we are now serving the world, serving God's children wherever we can reach them.

I always wanted God to give me the world. Not the material world in its material vanity, but the world as the Broken Body of Christ. I wanted the world to minister to it, to bring it God's Healing, to serve as humble intercessor between God's Grace and man's eternal need.

Now God is answering my plea. Through His manifestations, and under the control and guidance of my superiors, I am serving the world.

All glory to God, Creator of the world, Author of our lives, Maker of Ralph DiOrio, the man beneath the Gift, and the One and Only Heart of the Gift Itself.

Praise God. Amen.

❖